TOM MIX
RIDING UP TO GLORY

Best Wishes
Tom Mix
140

TOM MIX

RIDING UP TO GLORY

By John H. Nicholas

Introduction by Gene Autry

A Persimmon Hill Book

Front jacket illustration: Tom Mix by Lajos Markos; oil on canvas, 36 x 28 inches.
Copyright ©1978 National Cowboy Hall of Fame and Western Heritage Center Collection

All photographs from the collection of the author unless otherwise credited.

FIRST EDITION
Copyright ©1980 National Cowboy Hall of Fame and
Western Heritage Center, Oklahoma City, Oklahoma

L.C. 80-81554   ISBN 0-932154-05-0

Printed in the United States of America
by The Lowell Press, Inc., Kansas City, Missouri.

Dedicated to:

My wife, Mary; my parents, Harry Nicholas and the late Helen Nicholas; my in-laws, Ethel and the late George Vanezalos, and my wife's grandparents, Mr. and Mrs. S. Queses. Our daughters and sons-in-law, Helen and Paul, Ethel and Arthur; our grandchildren, Christ, Arthur, Mary and Alexandria. Tom Mix's daughter, Mrs. Ruth Mix Hill, and his grandchildren, Mrs. Tomasita Hill Lipe, William Hickman Hill and Gordon Hill.

Acknowledgments

To Odie Faulk for his good advice, assistance and encouragement; John Zois, of the Detroit Greek Program, for his fine comments on his radio hour; William T. Noble of the *Detroit News;* Carl Pavsner and Manuel L. Papista, for their advice and encouragement.

Contents

Mix and Autry in the Hollywood Christmas parade, 1939.

Introduction

Tom Mix has always been one of my idols. When I first started in the motion picture business, he treated me kindly from the beginning. The fact that he had gotten his start in show business in Oklahoma with the Miller Brothers' 101 and I was from Oklahoma was a definite plus for me.

Tom had affection for Oklahoma and had learned his great horsemanship there under the tutelage of the Millers. Will Rogers had been at the 101 Ranch at the same time, as had Lucille Mulhall, who was probably the greatest female performer in the history of rodeo and Wild West-type shows. Tom loved to reminisce about the Millers, Lucille, and Will Rogers.

When sound came to the motion picture screen, it was a blow to Tom as well as to many others and they had a tough time adjusting to it. That was about the time I started in pictures and brought in the new era of the singing cowboy.

The first time I met Tom Mix was back in about 1931 or '32. At that time I was on radio in Chicago on Station WLS and I was making a personal appearance around Peoria, Illinois, and Tom was appearing with the Sells-Floto Circus. Then later I met him when he was appearing with his own circus and Dale Turney and Johnny Agee, who both later worked for me, also worked for Tom at that time.

Several years later I was in the Hollywood Christmas Parade with Tom and I recall riding side by side with him. I remember how flashy he dressed and the big white Stetson he always wore. In my opinion Tom Mix was the greatest showman of all the western stars in that era and did more to bring the real West to the screen than anyone else in his time. He was a fine horseman and also did many of his own stunts and always looked the part in the saddle.

At one time he commanded the highest salary in western pictures—$10,000 a week—but like so many of the stars of that time, his worst fault, if he had one, was that he did not take care of his money. Perhaps he was too generous and he always lived first class—high and mighty.

It was 1940 and Tom had been in El Paso to visit some of his old buddies and on his way back he stopped off in Tucson to visit a mutual friend of ours, Sheriff Ed Eckles. Then he headed for Phoenix, driving his big white Packard convertible. They had a flash flood in the desert which had washed out a bridge near Florence, Arizona. Tom was driving too fast to stop in time and was killed. There is still a marker there where the accident occurred and the spot is called "Tom Mix Gulch."

I'm pleased that John Nicholas has written this straightforward biography of Tom Mix. He tells of Mix the way I remember him. He was a true son of the Old West.

GENE AUTRY
Honorary Chairman of the Board of Directors
National Cowboy Hall of Fame

x

Author's Foreword

I first saw Tom Mix at a matinee theater in Detroit, Michigan. I was among a thousand or more youngsters who came that day to see a living legend. Although this occurred more than fifty years ago, I remember how he looked: he was wearing his big white hat, his neckerchief had a knot tied sideways, his shirt had fancy embroidering, and he wore pearl-handled six-shooters in holsters on his hips. His Western trousers were snug-fitting, and his brightly stitched boots must have cost a fortune. This was an unforgettable thrill for me, one I will never forget.

My parents had come from Greece, and times had been difficult for them and their family. For us, Tom Mix *was* the dream of America. He was part of the lure of the West which, like Buffalo Bill, had won the hearts of millions in both the Old and New World. Seeing Tom Mix, getting to wave at him, shouting his name on that cold Saturday morning—all this did something to me. It gave me a hope of bettering myself, and it implanted in me a love of the West that has endured. Unlike many of the thousands of youngsters in that crowd, I did not and could not forget Tom Mix. I lay awake at night thinking about him, about his great horse Tony, and about his movies. He was my idol both in fancy and fact, and I vowed I would do more than cherish his memory. I swore that Mix's life and his "code of the range" would be guidelines for my life—as much as was possible in Detroit.

Moreover, without realizing it, I became a student of the life of this great movie star. With the pennies and nickels I saved, I bought whatever pictures I could find of him in order to gain insights into his life and adventures. I read books and magazines that mentioned him even in the slightest way. At times I considered writing him a letter, but felt too insignificant and too far removed from him to do it. Because of my devotion to Mix, I was the butt of many jokes from my contemporaries, who often called me "Tom Mix, Junior" or "Tony Junior." Even my parents discouraged me, but my obsession grew until it became far more than a hobby. It became the world I lived in.

Time has not diminished my enchantment with Tom Mix. For more than fifty years, my collection has grown to number in the thousands of items. My library of books, magazine articles, and clippings is comprehensive, and I have many reels of his films. Across the years my devotion to Tom Mix has been shared by my wife, Mary, and our daughters, Helen and Ethel. Moreover, my research has brought us dozens of new friends. I have corresponded with Mrs. Olive Mix, his relatives, his children, and his boyhood friends. I have become acquainted with people who worked with him on and off the stage. My interest has taken me to all the places he lived, from his birthplace in Pennsylvania, to Oklahoma where his career began, to the motion picture studios and lots in Hollywood, to the National Cowboy Hall of Fame and Western Heritage Center where he is an honoree in the Hall of Fame of Great Western Performers, to the place in Arizona where he met his tragic and untimely death.

When, in 1940, I learned that he had been killed, I was stunned. I felt like I had lost a member of my family—perhaps more, for he had inspired me to be "a good man, a straight-shooter in life, a true-blue Westerner."

Forty years have passed since Tom Mix died, and a new generation has come into the world—a generation with its own heroes, a generation not privileged to see in person or on the screen the man my generation did, a man like Mix who was devoted to his audiences and his image, a man who felt his moral responsibilities and who often said, "I want to keep my pictures in such a vein that parents will not object to letting their children see me on the screen."

Tom Mix has been remembered in many ways, but his real monument is the memories which millions of Americans carry in their minds of a man known as the "King of the Cowboys." It is not my intent here to write a full biography of Tom Mix, for I am not a biographer. Rather I will leave behind my large collection of pictures, my catalog of Mixiana, and my memorabilia. Most of all, I want to leave a bit of the spirit and admiration I hold. There is nothing wrong with hero worship. I believe our young people need someone to whom they can give their admiration; this is desperately needed today. In addition, I hope that this work will serve to perpetuate the memory of Tom Mix and Tony, who should continue to ride up to glory through the ages. The image should always be fresh and their films always loved. This is my story of Tom Mix.

John H. Nicholas

Cast and camera crew, circa 1919. Tom Mix is seated center, front

right is Sid Jordan.

right is Sid Jordan.

Chapter 1

PENNSYLVANIA

After Tom Mix became a movie idol, promotion men, publicity agents, and writers tried to locate his birthplace somewhere in the American West. However, he was born on January 6, 1880 at Mix Run, which is in the heart of the coal mining country in Cameron County, Pennsylvania. The nearest town of any size was DuBois. His father was Edwin Elias Mix and his mother Mary Elizabeth (Heistand) Mix. Named Thomas Edwin Mix, he was the second son in a family that would number four children. His father was a native of Mix Run, while his mother had been born and raised at Marietta in Lancaster County, Pennsylvania. About 1888 the Mix family moved to DuBois, where his father became coachman and later superintendent of the stables for John E. DuBois, a giant in the lumbering industry.

Little is known of Tom Mix's early childhood except that he loved the out-of-doors. He enjoyed camping out, hiking through the woods, and working with animals. From his father he learned a love of horses that lasted through his lifetime.

The Pennsylvania of Tom Mix's childhood was not far removed from the days of the Civil War and the great Battle of Gettysburg. Also part of his heritage in that region were stories of the great migration westward through Pennsylvania as pioneers fought the Indians for mastery of the Ohio Valley, Tennessee, and Kentucky. Historic Fort Pitt intrigued the young lad, while nearby Lancaster, Pennsylvania had been the site of the manufacture of the famous Conestoga wagon, the ship of the desert.

Much that is untrue has been written of Tom's boyhood—stories that he could stick to a horse's back and, at ten, could nick a bottle with a rifle at fifty paces; that when he was seven, he took part in a circus knife-throwing act; and at eight, after his parents took him to Waring, Tennessee, he worked in a blacksmith shop for thirty cents a week.

When Mix was ten years old, the last major engagement between the Sioux Indians and the United States Cavalry occurred. This was the battle at Wounded Knee at the Pine Ridge Indian Agency in South Dakota. Later Tom would talk personally with men who had participated in this tragic affair, both soldiers and Indians. He had a deep sense of history which he carried through life and, as he aged, he became more appreciative of the spirit that had moved pioneers to go west.

Tom Mix was not studious and meditative as a lad. He disliked books and the confinement of the schoolroom, preferring to watch his father work with horses. Few men were as adept at handling these animals. Mix later would recall, "Dad could do about anything with a horse, except make him speak." From his father he gained not only his love of horses but also his great knowledge about them. By the time he arrived in his early teens, Mix was an expert horseman. He could ride and rope, just as he could shoe, harness, and doctor a horse, as well as handle a six-team hookup on a freight wagon. His early life revolved around horses—his first and greatest love. On his horses Tom Mix was to win the hearts of Americans, earn his millions of dollars, and ride up to glory.

Another great influence on the life and outlook of Tom Mix was Buffalo Bill Cody and the showmanship associated with the Wild West Show. As a lad, Tom Mix read the stories spread by Cody's press agents, and these fired his imagination. He soon formed a desire to be part of

Buffalo Bill's Wild West Show and Congress of Rough Riders—a desire as strong as his wish to claim Cherokee Indian ancestry and his yearning to have been born in Texas. Thus he and his playmates at DuBois rehearsed the equestrian acts and routines of the Wild West Show in local lots and corrals, just as they tried to learn trick shooting. Tom's mother would shake her head and wonder what the future might hold for a boy who cared little about traditional chores and work.

Tom Mix was a child of difficult times and parents of limited means. However, he was not without dreams. As a son, he was an economic asset that could be farmed out to supplement the family's income, and he was used as an aid to his father. However, during these years he was given an opportunity to develop a sterling character and a strong, well-coordinated body. His father's abilities as a handler and trainer of horses provided a discipline to the youngster, as did the daylight-to-dark routine of doing chores over and over until perfection was achieved. To this discipline and constant effort to achieve perfection in handling animals, Mix added his own ingredients: showmanship, drama, and poise. He was termed "a natural." Early in life he learned that a horse could easily be sold if it was taught to prance, change its gait, kneel, and shake its head when commanded to do so by a slight pressure from the rider's knees or a softly voiced command.

Unlike his brother and sisters, Tom was not a socializer or pal. Instead he developed his own likes and dislikes, and he was a competitor—not in the sense of wanting to make a team but rather in wanting to be a man when he was yet a boy. He worked, thought, and acted like a man when he was only sixteen. According to those who knew him at this period, he cared little for sentimental things in life, such as family outings, picnics, and holidays. He became a loner, seeking recognition and the better things of life. The glimpse of glamor he received when Buffalo Bill came to town was the sort of life he aspired to; perhaps this was a conscious yearning, but without doubt the visit of the Wild West Show to him was an emotional experience. Like Cody, he was adventurous, but his experiences would have to be drawn from a different era.

Despite his strength of character and his determination to go far in life, Tom Mix in some ways was his mother's child. From her he gained his sense of fair play and his spirit of Christianity which he voiced in public after he achieved stardom. And it was his mother's gentleness which gave him pride and humility.

In the makeup of Tom Mix were many characteristics that pointed him toward stardom, but few as important as his appearance and his good looks. He was a fine physical specimen, standing just under five feet, eleven inches in height with big shoulders, a broad chest, and narrow hips. His years in the saddle endowed him with a cavalryman's physique. He had powerful arms and strong hands, both toughened by roping and handling harness and reins. In his face he resembled Rudolph Valentino somewhat. His complexion was dark, his hair wavy and black, his nose aquiline, and his ears well formed. Especially noteworthy were his eyes, which were dark with heavy brows above them. D. W. Griffith, the great movie director, once commented, "Mix could burn a hole through a camera lens by merely staring at it if he wanted to. When he looked at you, you were being looked at." There was a set to his jaw and mouth that showed firmness and a strong will. As he became an adult, Mix was gaining a masculine appearance, although it would be several years before he realized the importance of this image.

His greatest facial asset was his broad smile. When his white teeth flashed, the world smiled with him. Mix had a soft, resonant voice that caused people to listen. In time he would develop a slight drawl, that of the Southwest.

Good looks were Mix's greatest asset and made him a center of attention almost from the beginning of his life. He would retain his poise, his physical ability, and his good looks into middle age. These would help him win fame and earn millions, and brought him a succession of beautiful women—along with much of the heartache and personal tragedy which life would deal him.

Chapter 2

YOUNG CAVALIER

One dictionary defines a cavalier as "horseman; knight; lover; escort." Tom Mix embodied and exemplified the attributes of a cavalier—and more.

When Tom Mix first considered leaving home, he apparently thought of joining the navy. Luckily for him, however, the navy refused to accept him. Had it done so, he doubtless would have been assigned to sea duty. This would have been bad for Mix, for he was a born cavalryman. A life in the saddle was his past and his future; duty at sea might have derailed his climb to stardom. Yet Mix was thinking seriously about a tour of military duty, for world events were drawing the United States toward war as he approached his eighteenth birthday.

Little did Mix or other Americans realize the significance of the Cuban rebellion against Spain which began in 1895. For three years, the conflict raged between Spaniards and insurgents. American investments in Cuba, estimated at fifty million dollars, suffered, while the destruction of sugar and tobacco crops by the insurgents reduced trade between the United States and Cuba to a vanishing point. Americans drifted toward involvement in the war more for moral reasons than any property damage, however. Americans sympathized with the Cubans, who were fighting for their independence from Spain and an end to the cruel treatment which had been their lot. By early 1898, newspapers across the United States were clamoring for intervention. Then, on February 15, 1898, came the blowing up of the battleship *Maine* in the harbor at Havana. Americans were outraged, and diplomatic relations were severed between the two countries, ending with a declaration of war on April 21.

This excitement stirred Tom Mix (now eighteen) who yearned for adventure. Refused by the navy, he enlisted in the army. His mother wanted him to stay home, but no amount of pleading could sway her handsome son. Volunteering for action, he rode off—for a lifetime of adventure.

Tom's background qualified him for the artillery as a handler of horses and a commander of men. Sent to Fort Sam Houston, Texas, he was attached to one of the most celebrated regiments in American military history, the cavalry unit that became known as the Rough Riders. Among those organizing this unit were Colonel Leonard Wood and Lieutenant Colonel Theodore Roosevelt.

After a brief period of training at Fort Sam Houston, the regiment boarded troop trains for Tampa, Florida, the port of embarkation. According to newspaper correspondent Richard Harding Davis, the embarkation was "one of vast confusion." Space was available aboard ships for only about half the regiment, forcing those in command to begin weeding out the "men from the boys." No one could deny that Tom Mix was a man, and he was among those chosen for the campaign. However, there was no room for the horses.

Mix was disappointed that the mounts had to be left behind, but like his comrades, he was excited at the prospect of going into battle. The fragment of the First Cavalry that finally engaged the enemy at Las Guasimas, led by Colonel Wood, was discouraged in every way save fighting spirit. The Rough Riders had little problem in routing the enemy. As a result of this battle, Leonard Wood was promoted to brigadier general, and Theodore Roosevelt was elevated to full colonel. During this campaign, as the unit became better organized, Tom Mix was made a

During Spanish-American War, 1898 (age 18).

Fourth Regiment, United States Artillery, 1898. Mix is seated center, front row.

scout and courier for Generals Wheeler and Chaffee.

After the withdrawal of Spaniards from the outpost at Las Guasimas in June 1898, the key defenses for the Spanish-held town of Santiago, Cuba were elsewhere. One major point was San Juan Hill, which lay to the northeast of El Canay; San Juan Hill was directly in the path of the American advance, while El Canay protected the city from envelopment by the American right flank.

On July 1 the American attack began. A force led by General Henry Lawton carried El Canay, but the attack on San Juan Hill was not well timed. The Rough Riders were part of the force that pushed up this high ground, the advance made as much from desperation as by design. By sheer bravery, the Rough Riders overran the hill, thereby giving the American force control of the high ground overlooking the city of Santiago and put them in a position to isolate it. During this advance, Tom Mix received a serious and unusual wound. A bullet passed through a portion of his neck. He was rushed to a field hospital where he received first aid, then was transferred to a hospital aboard ship. Within a matter of weeks, Private Mix was on his feet again and ready for

more action—only to learn that the war was virtually over.

While Mix was recuperating from his wound, Spanish Admiral Pascual Cervera, fearing American shelling from the high ground, attempted to escape to the safety of the high seas. Admiral William T. Sampson, commander of the American naval forces, gave battle and destroyed the Spanish fleet. Spanish officials at Santiago were so disheartened by this action that on July 17, 1898, they surrendered. This effectively ended fighting in Cuba.

While Americans were celebrating this victory, Tom Mix was aboard a troop transport and soon steaming for the Philippines. The first soldiers had sailed from San Francisco late in June just as Cuba's fate was determined. Mix arrived in the Philippines in time to participate in the battles against the insurgents who fought American control, a fight that began on February 4, 1899. This campaign largely was commanded by Brigadier General Arthur McArthur.

On the ship from San Francisco to the Philippines, Tom Mix found he was a hero. Nothing gives a soldier more prestige than a wound gained in battle, and he was the center of attention. He had looked death in the eye and had won. This was the beginning of what some people later would call "Tom Mix luck."

Private Mix's career in the Philippines was noteworthy. He participated in the shelling of Manila. In fact, during this battle he witnessed the explosion of a shell held by a member of the battery. This tragic scene of a soldier holding his hands, half torn off, over his face while bleeding and screaming, staggering blindly about minutes before death, never left Tom Mix. Later he would urge the director producing the film version of the great novel of World War I, *All Quiet on the Western Front,* to recreate the scene.

Mix's life suddenly changed direction in May 1900, when his artillery unit was assigned to a detachment of approximately 2,500 men being sent to China. In that nation, a group of nationalists, known as Boxers, had decided to drive all foreigners out of the country or else exterminate them. Several hundred foreigners, including many Americans, had been killed, while in Peking the British legation (wherein many foreigners had taken refuge) was under siege.

Mix was assigned to a Gardner gun crew attached to the Ninth Infantry. This unit, along with a contingent of British and French forces, soon was in battle. During one skirmish, Tom Mix received a superficial wound on the forehead. Although the wound was not critical, he was taken out of action, put aboard ship, and sent home to the United States. The young cavalier, although hardly twenty, had seen his share of action and the world.

Fate decreed that he was to see more of the world, however. Promoted to corporal, he was assigned to accompany a shipment of saddle horses to South Africa, horses which had been purchased by the British government in its war with the Boers. Mix witnessed the battles between these two forces at Ladysmith and Spinecob. This war proved exciting—and tragic—for Mix and his fellow Americans. For Mix, the pain was in seeing the loss and suffering of cavalry horses he had helped train, as well as witnessing the death of so many humans.

Tom Mix returned to the United States in 1902 for discharge. At age twenty-two, he was a veteran and world traveler, a cavalier who knew the limits of his courage. The Orient had afforded him a glimpse of life that he would see nowhere else, for there he viewed a low regard for human life. He had seen splendor and elegance as well. This had been his education. He had tasted life's fruits, and he knew that life was what he might make of it. He could aspire to elegance and splendor or sink to suffering and degradation. Above all, he knew that at last he was a man, and as Will Rogers said, "a damn good one!"

One aspect of this period of Mix's life would remain with him: his pride in being part of the Rough Riders. Colonel Theodore Roosevelt had returned from the war to be elected governor of New York in 1898 and vice-president of the United States in 1900. Following the assassination of President William McKinley, Roosevelt had become chief executive of the United States. Across the years, the president participated in the reunions of the Rough Riders, which also were meaningful in the life of Tom Mix. His heritage as part of the Rough Riders, a group that in many ways symbolized the new America, was interwoven into the fabric of his own daring life.

Chapter 3

MAGIC OF THE ARENA

Much has been written about Tom Mix's activities between his discharge from the army and his entrance into Wild West shows, but little of this has been documented. Press agents later would write of his chasing notorious outlaws, exchanging shots with them at close range, supervising hangings, and spilling blood in general. However, there is little evidence to support such statements, just as there is scant documentation that he was a full-fledged Texas Ranger patroling the Rio Grande.

Tom Mix was an adventurer, and he perhaps was a bounty hunter and member of a posse on occasion. He did know the Southwest, particularly Texas, having trained in San Antonio prior to the war in Cuba. However, his career as a lawman, if genuine, was brief, for he soon gravitated to the world of show business. From the vantage point of history, this move on his part seems inevitable, for it was one of growth along natural lines.

The Oklahoma Territory was home to several Wild West shows, a part of show business catering to the American desire to see cowboys and Indians and to witness the gunfights so luridly described by dime novelists of the day. One such show, as well as working ranch, was owned by Colonel Zack Mulhall. It was his show that attracted Tom Mix to Oklahoma, for Mulhall needed cowboys, ropers, and trick shots for his pageant of the Old West which he intended to take to the St. Louis World's Fair in 1904.

When he arrived at Mulhall's ranch, Tom Mix was a showman's dream. He had everything a man like Mulhall and his brother needed: Mix was young, handsome, daring, seasoned in battle, and one of the best horsemen the colonel had ever seen. Moreover, Mix could shoot and twirl a Mexican maguey rope with fancy dexterity.

Will Rogers was another performer who, like Tom Mix, got his start in show business with Colonel Zack Mulhall. In fact, Rogers and Mix became close friends, and from the bond of their common humble beginnings grew a lifelong admiration for one another. In his autobiography, Will Rogers told of his start in show business and of the Mulhall troupe:

My real show career kinder dates from the time I first run into Colonel Zack Mulhall. It was in 1899 at the St. Louis Fair (not World's Fair), just the big St. Louis Fair they held every year. They decided as an attraction that they would put on a roping contest. They were not called rodeos or stampedes in those days. They were just what they are: a roping and riding contest. Well, I was pretty much a kid, but just happened to have won the first and only contest at home in Claremore, Oklahoma and then we read about them wanting entries for this big contest at St. Louis.

Well, someone sent in my name, and the first thing I knew I was getting transportation for myself and pony to the affair. Well, I went and Colonel Zack Mulhall had charge of it. I didn't get very far in the St. Louis contest. I made the serious mistake of catching my steer, and he immediately jerked me and my pony down, for our trouble.

But it gave me a touch of "show business" in a way, so that meant I was ruined for life as far as actual employment was concerned....

Rogers, in this same book, gave an insight into the budding career of Tom Mix:

PRINCE FOTOGRAFER. TOM MIX MUSEUM, OKLAHOMA HISTORICAL SOCIETY

Then, the following year, about 1903 [sic], Colonel Zack Mulhall brought a bunch of us boys to New York from the West to give an exhibition in Madison Square Garden.

Tom Mix was with us. That was his first start on his Wild West career. We didn't get much money; in fact, our salary was supposed to be twenty dollars a week. That was one time we were not overpaid actors, because we didn't even get the twenty.

The Mulhall Wild West Show enjoyed a brief but colorful history. From it, Tom Mix received a taste of the life he was to grow to love and lead. His friendship with Rogers was an enduring one, something kept private across the years and seldom known by the public. Aside from their humble origins in show business in Oklahoma, the two men had much in common.

As a result of his appearance in Madison Square Garden, Will Rogers went on to the bright lights of Broadway to star in productions of the Ziegfield Follies. Then came fame and fortune. For Tom Mix, the road to success was slower and more difficult than for his rope-twirling, gum-chewing, wisecracking friend.

From the small operation and unpredictable schedule of Zack Mulhall, Tom Mix in 1906 moved to the well-organized and well-financed show of the Miller Brothers and their 101 Ranch near Ponca City, Oklahoma. He was signed as a cowboy and stock handler. This ranch and its Wild West show constituted a fascinating epoch of the opportunity available in the Old West.

Moving west from Kentucky in 1871, Colonel George Washington Miller arrived in Kansas where, through trading, he acquired title to twenty thousand pounds of bacon. With this he went south to San Saba County, Texas, where he swapped the bacon for four hundred longhorn steers. These he drove to the northeastern part of the Indian Territory and sold to the Quapaw Indians for a handsome profit. Then, moving to the Cherokee Outlet, he leased sixty thousand acres and began stocking his range with Texas longhorns. Next he persuaded the Ponca Indians to accept a reservation near his leased land, and he persuaded them to allow him to graze his cattle on their land for one-cent-a-year-per-acre rent. He proved an excellent friend of the tribe, and when they were forced to accept allotments,

Captain Seth Bullock's Cowboy Brigade at second inauguration of Theodore Roosevelt, March 1905. Mix is third from right, front row.

he bought land from them until the ranch included 101 sections of land owned outright.

By the time George Miller died in 1903, his 101 Ranch had thirteen thousand acres sown in wheat, three thousand acres in corn, and three thousand acres in forage crops. He died in the dugout that had been the ranch headquarters since its start, but the three-story "White House" headquarters was completed shortly after his death.

Inheriting the ranch were his three sons, Joseph C., Zack T., and George L. Joe, as the oldest son, assumed the leadership, although his major interest was in the Wild West show which was formed about 1905. Like his father, Joe proved a good friend of the Ponca Indians, who adopted him into the tribe and eventually made him their official chief.

Zack, the second son, assisted with the 101 Wild West Show. In addition, he was in charge of the livestock on the ranch and made outside purchases and trades. George, the youngest son, was the financial agent for the operation and provided the managerial skills needed for such a vast operation. When oil and gas were discovered on the property, George became heavily involved with E. W. Marland, founder of Marland Oil Company (later to be part of Conoco). Together the three sons built the 101 Ranch into a major empire that included 101,000 acres of land, twenty-five thousand cattle, three hundred miles of fence, two hundred and fifty employees, an electric power plant, a canning plant, a cotton gin, a tannery, a cider mill, an alfalfa mill, a modern dairy and poultry department, a meat packing plant with cold storage facilities, a community store, a restaurant, and a small refinery to produce their own gasoline, kerosene, and fuel oil.

The 101 brand was applied to their horses and cattle, as well as to their stationery, posters, saddles, and firearms. In fact, the brand became one of the best known in the West, standing for quality and success.

Because so many cowboys and Indians were at the ranch, they frequently were called upon to demonstrate their skills, and people began flocking to the White House to watch. In 1905 Joe Miller invited the National Editorial Association to hold its annual meeting at the ranch—and to his astonishment, a total of sixty thousand people arrived. For these guests the cowboys and Indians demonstrated their abilities and skills. The Millers did not refer to this as a rodeo or as a show; rather, they called it a "roundup." The editors were so enthusiastic in their praise that the Miller Brothers decided to take the show on tour—and thus was born their Wild West show. When the Jamestown Exposition was held at Norfolk, Virginia in 1907, President Theodore Roosevelt invited the Millers to display their show there.

The 1907 season gave Tom Mix confidence in his ability. Although he did not receive top billing, he was able to develop into a professional performer; he learned the Millers' routines, and he gained experience. Almost without conscious effort, he showed an ease and grace in the saddle that brought forth applause. Moreover, his ability to handle whatever horse he happened to be riding pleased his employers. In the center of the arena, he appeared relaxed, although inside he was filled with excitement. And he discovered that he loved the crowds, and he tried to please them. If this was show business, he loved it.

Among the performers in the Miller show with whom Tom would become a lifelong friend was Texas-born Leonard Stroud. As a young man, Stroud earned a reputation for his daring and able riding and roping. Early in his career he was recognized as a champion trick rider. From him, Tom Mix learned many of the tricks that would make him famous in the movies—including Mix's ability to swing under the belly of a horse moving at full gallop.

Another great rodeo performer Mix observed in the 101 show was Bill Pickett, the famous black cowboy. Pickett was credited with originating the art of bulldogging, now considered one of the major events of the rodeo. One feat Pickett often demonstrated was throwing a steer by leaping on it like a bulldogger, then biting the steer on its lip and throwing it to the ground. This trick, along with Pickett's ability to bulldog a buffalo, made him a featured performer in the show.

Mix studied all the performers, both stars and unknowns, and from them he learned many tricks. A tireless worker with great self-discipline, he wanted to excel as a performer. As he studied and worked to perfect his own skills, he little realized that he was perfecting his abilities for the movies.

Chapter 4
ON CAMERA

Little did Tom Mix realize in 1910 that his life was about to change dramatically. He had no thought of becoming a motion picture star or of pioneering in the development of that industry, but such was to be his role. That year the infant film industry was sputtering along. No central home for it had been found, and the making of pictures was a hit-or-miss proposition. Companies were formed, pictures were made practically anywhere, the producer tried to arrange distribution, and money was made—or lost. Tom Mix would do much to stabilize the industry and make it profitable.

No one could have foreseen his role in 1910 when Colonel William Selig came to the 101 Ranch to make a one-reel film entitled, *Ranch Life in the Great Southwest*. Its purpose was to show how beef cattle were raised and marketed. Wanting to add a bit of excitement to the film, Selig introduced the matter of rustling as a realistic problem in the story of ranching. Mix, as foreman of the 101, was the logical "star," while ordinary cowboys played the roles of rustlers. As the episode developed, Mix saved the herd by fancy shooting and trick riding.

The Chicagoans were astonished at what Mix did, for the shooting of firearms was done with real bullets, not blanks and trick photography. The script called for nothing like what they saw, while the strong, silent Mix seemed not to be acting, not just doing what the director wanted, but actually living the part. Then, for an encore, Mix put on a riding exhibition, including a stirrup dance, that left director Francis Boggs and the film crew gasping.

The filming completed, the production crew returned to Chicago while Mix continued his work at the 101, thinking merely that making a film had been an interesting distraction. However, when the film was processed, Selig saw great possibilities in the good looks and raw talent of the 101's foreman. Public reaction to the film confirmed this belief. Mix, meanwhile, had quit the 101 and had gone down to the Mexican border country looking for excitement and bounty money tracking down outlaws. It was almost a year before he returned to the Miller Ranch to discover that Colonel Selig had been looking for him with a job offer.

Arriving in Chicago, Mix learned that Selig had many things for him to do for the company. In addition to doing all the trick riding and roping, all the stunts, and taking all the falls, he was to manage both domestic and wild animals and train the horses. His ability to perform as an extra, to double for other actors, and to work before the camera soon put the lead actors "in the shade," and he quickly became a regular in Selig productions. One of his first films as a star was *Back to the Primitive*.

By the end of 1910, Tom Mix had become a major figure at Selig. The company had set up a studio in West Los Angeles, and there Mix found himself creating dialog, outlining situations and scenes, and directing the action. However, he was uncertain about continuing in the film industry despite the moderate success of Selig films. For example, in 1911 he and a former cowboy at the 101 Ranch, Guy Weadick, went to Calgary, Canada to try to organize a rodeo in the Canadian West. The effort failed, and both men lost their financial shirts. Mix thereupon returned to California, but Weadick remained in Canada, gained the necessary financial backing, and started one of the great rodeos of North America, the Calgary Stampede. Tom Mix joined Ma-

TOM MIX
SELIG PLAYER

dero's forces in Mexico, and for a while he faced a firing squad only to be saved when it became known that the charges against him were false.

By 1912 Selig and his crew had refined their techniques of film making and had improved their productions. Mix, thirty-two years old, decided to become serious about his acting career. The scripts he received generally were simple outlines; to these he added his own theatrics and expressive actions. By 1913 he had made seven films, mostly one-reel each. That year he would add *The Escape of Jim Dolan, Child of the Prairie,* and *Law and Outlaw.*

These productions were popular silents and played to audiences throughout America in poorly lighted theaters. Acting and expression had to carry the plot while simple dialog flashed on the screen periodically as the story unfolded. Most theaters had a pianist who played tunes that emphasized the mood of what was occurring on screen. Frequently these showings were interrupted as film broke or the projector malfunctioned, and the audience would shout its disappointment and dismay when these occurred. The children would huddle around one of their number who could read.

The art of making motion pictures was evolving during this era, and Tom Mix was a part of the pioneering effort. Action scenes often were poorly shot, moving at an accelerated pace. Film historians usually note that Selig was a humorist who, on occasion, attempted to bring the problems of production into his films and onto the screen, a technique that mystified his audiences. Yet this pioneer firm popularized the Saturday afternoon kids' matinee and made the Saturday evening show for mother and father something special.

By 1914 Selig and Mix began to hit their stride, producing an average of one film per month. For the most part these were two-reelers, each lasting about fifteen minutes. Mix's best role that year was in the film version of B. M. Bowers' book, *Chip of the Flying U.* Set in Montana, the book had appeared in 1904 and was one of the country's best-liked range romances. Tom Mix played the role of Chip, an affable fellow similar to the Virginian in his sense of honor, and in the process won his way into Americans' hearts. The success of this film reinforced some film producers' belief in the worth of a good story in making a good film.

Film historians George N. Fenin and William K. Everson, in their excellent book, *The Western—From Silents to Cinerama,* summarized Mix's career with Selig:

Although the Mix period with Selig was generally uneventful, this was due more to company policy than to any shortcomings on the part of Mix. Selig was mostly interested in and geared for the production of shorts, limiting Mix to one, two and three reelers. Committed to quantity, he had no time to develop his own screen personality or to enlarge the scope of films themselves. Nevertheless, the films proved to be useful training ground for Mix, and they did improve as they went along. When he joined Fox in 1917, there was no uncertainty or faltering. He became an immediate star attraction.

Fox, like Selig, was located in a metropolitan area. It was founded on Staten Island, New York then moved into Manhattan offices in 1916, while the production part of the studio followed the sun to southern California. The driving force behind the studio was William Fox, a pioneer in the early days of the film industry. He was a contemporary of such illustrious men as D. W. Griffith, Jesse Laskey, and Cecil B. DeMille.

When Tom Mix decided he wanted to work for Fox, he tried to get the owner's attention by being conspicuous. William Fox later recalled, "Every morning for a week this same person [Tom Mix] was waiting near the studio door, always in a different Western costume, each one more garish than the last. Finally, I approached this person who introduced himself as Tom Mix."

Film historians Fenin and Everson declare that Mix's real career began when Fox signed him in 1917. Fox was better organized than Selig and saw the film industry in a much broader light. Fox had specialists in each of the important areas of production: script writing, costuming, filming, film direction, production, editing, distribution, and promotion. Moreover, Fox knew how to handle his star, Tom Mix, like Mix knew how to handle horses—at times Fox would be gentle, at other times he would snub him. When it came to shooting a picture, however, Fox recalled, "I'd pull his bridle off and swat Mix on the rump, and away he went, putting his heart and soul into his work."

Tom Mix thereby became the person he had dreamed of being: the real Tom Mix, the Tom Mix of fiction and fantasy in a celluloid nevernever land. He became whatever the script called for—anything but a kid from the unglamorous, unromantic coal mining country of Pennsylvania.

Mix arrived on the scene with Fox just as the film industry needed a new cowboy image to replace the aging and overly dramatic William S. Hart. Mix had served his apprenticeship at Selig. He could ride and shoot, and he could act. At Fox he found almost everything he did regulated and controlled, but the young man from DuBois was prepared to become the Cadillac Cowboy.

Chapter 5
CADILLAC COWBOY

Tom Mix rose to stardom for many reasons, but none was as significant as his being on the scene at precisely the right moment. His achievement of status as a star was not based on any long-range plan or study or self-discipline, much less a devotion to the movie industry or to acting. He merely had found acting before the cameras to be a way of making a living, and for several years he had moved in and out of the film

world as casually as he had in the field of law enforcement and ranching.

At first he merely had tasted the fruits of fame. Suddenly, however, it overwhelmed him. At first he remained a nonchalant cowboy, the same fellow who had been foreman of the 101 Ranch. He prided himself on his background as an authentic cowboy, one who had slept in a bedroll, broken horses, and ridden in a roundup. Gradually he was swept along the Hollywood road of the unreal and became lost in the tinsel and glitter of success. Ultimately he would demand luxury and all the trappings that went with being a star. Not even the birth of his daughter would slow the growth of his ego; instead, he demanded for his new offspring all the gifts and attention that money and status could buy.

The first tie with the past that he broke was his marriage to Olive Stokes, the beautiful girl from Oklahoma who had shared with him those early days in films. She had starred in his first films, had coached, schooled and tutored him, and had helped him in many ways. She had wanted Tom to settle down and become a family man, but this was not a part of the new world he was entering. Olive Mix represented the past: the bedrolls, the branding corrals, and the bunk house. Their marriage lasted from 1909 to 1917. Mix left her with wealth, but somewhat forsaken.

In 1917 Mix married the attractive Victoria Forde, the sister of director Gene Forde and one of the first actresses in the budding film industry. In fact, she had starred in some of Hollywood's earliest productions and had co-starred with Mix in some of his films. She and Mix were a hand-

Left: Victoria and Tom with Thomasina, 1922.
Right: Tom and Victoria Forde Mix.

16

some couple—busy, attractive, and living sumptuously to try to match their press agents' images of them. During these years Mix was still pliable (some detractors said he was unschooled). Too often he took the word and advice of his press agents when he should have spoken his own mind. Because of this, he began to confuse his role in real life as opposed to what he stood for on the screen. Nevertheless, the man with the million-dollar smile and the big white hat rode to new heights at Fox.

In part he became a major star because he was able to add realism to his acting roles, something that neither William S. Hart nor Bronco Billy Anderson had been able to bring to their portrayals on the screen. Mix would jump through windows, roll off roofs, jump or fall into the saddle, tumble a horse and roll with it, stand in the middle of a fusillade of bullets, or win in a barroom brawl. In short, he was unlike anything Hollywood—and the paying public—had ever seen. He was the iron man of the celluloid circus.

In addition, Tom Mix was popular with camera crews, who enjoyed working with him, just as did his women co-stars, some of whom were reported to have swooned in his arms. However, there were some producers who had different feelings about him. Because Mix made it a point to learn what went on behind the camera as well as in front of it, some producers felt threatened by him.

Whatever those in the front office at Fox Studios thought of Tom Mix, he easily was their biggest star. D. W. Griffith summarized one school of thought about the handsome cowboy star when he stated, "He can't act but he can ride like hell, and everybody loves him; I don't know why!"

In his first year at Fox, Mix emerged as actor, writer, and producer. One of his first important productions was *Six Cylinder Love,* followed by *Durrand of the Bad Lands, Six Shooter Andy,* and many others. The Fox Company was willing to enrich its productions by filming in beautiful natural settings, utilizing deserts, plains, and mountains.

Film historians have not always given Mix the credit he is due as one of the industry's most original thinkers. Unlike many of his contemporaries, he had experience in the Mulhall and 101 Ranch Wild West shows and was able to bring the concepts of action and drama he had learned there to the camera's eye. The concepts he innovated before the camera became the

A Ridin' Romeo, *1921.*

19

foundation of Western acting in the decades that followed.

In 1918, as the major star at Fox Studios, he continued to make their films adventurous and thrilling. Among his better-known movies that year were *Western Blood, Mr. Logan, U.S.A., Fame and Fortune, Treat 'Em Rough,* and *Ace High.* The following year saw him in *The Wilderness Trail, Hell Roarin' Reform, Fighting For Gold, Rough Riding Romance,* and *The Speed Maniac.* By this time Mix had developed his own film crews and his own unique style which accelerated production and brought his films in under budget. He could manage and oversee practically every phase of film making—but he could not contain the publicity and promotion given his personal life.

Tom Mix's salary by this time had risen to approximately seventeen thousand dollars per week, fifty-two weeks a year. This was an astronomical amount of money at that time; in fact, it was four times the salary of the president of the United States—in an era when the income tax was extremely low.

At the end of World War I, the United States went on what F. Scott Fitzgerald called "the gaudiest spree in history." Marathon dances, flagpole sitting, bobbed hair and short dresses for women were part of the new freedoms that were discovered; women won the right to vote, and some soon were smoking in public, drinking from

TOM MIX MUSEUM, OKLAHOMA HISTORICAL SOCIETY

flasks, and, in general, trying to keep up with men. America, it seemed, laughed more—and yearned for entertainment. The growing movie industry stood ready to feed the country's appetite. By 1922 approximately forty million movie tickets were sold weekly, a figure that by 1929 had doubled.

In this atmosphere Tom Mix emerged as the kingpin of Hollywood, and he lived in a style that befitted his position. At his home he developed a fine stable of horses, barns, feed lots, training corrals, and pastures. From this system he was able to bring to his films a touch of realism and appeal previously unknown. Moreover, he could contribute not only great horsemanship but also great horses with personality.

Mix's first great movie horse was Old Blue, a genuine cow pony he brought with him from Oklahoma to Hollywood. In an interview in *The New York Times* on July 12, 1925, Mix recalled Old Blue with affection, noting that it was this horse he rode to fame. He said that never did Old Blue's birthday arrive that he did not remember the horse and pay homage to him in some manner. When Old Blue was injured and had to be killed, Mix buried him in one of his corrals with a gravestone that stated, "In memory of Old Blue, the best horse I ever rode. Born July, 1897; killed January 29, 1919. We grew old together."

Long before Blue's death, Mix already was favoring a sorrel horse with a white diamond on his forehead and almost perfect white socks. His name was Tony. Foaled in California, Tony was of Hambletonian stock. Mix loved this animal and spent hours training and working with him. Eventually the horse learned to perform seemingly impossible tasks. Mix's devotion to the animal caused press agents at Fox to write endlessly about the relationship. These stories had wide appeal in an era when horses were becoming increasingly less important, and eventually the two, Mix and Tony, became inseparable images. The result was that horsemen and horse lovers flocked to Mix's pictures and gave him added strength at the box office.

Tony also became a regular part of Mix's personal appearances. When the two of them appeared, a crowd of thousands was certain to be there. These personal appearances became the most glamorous events that Hollywood public

Left: In the Days of the Thundering Herd, *1914.*
Right: Rescuing Kathleen Connors in Mr. Logan U.S.A., *1920.*

relations people could stage, and the public loved them. Mix would ride up on Tony, doff his large white hat, and flash his million-dollar smile, while Tony would respond to his rider's commands, given by knee pressure, and shake his head yes or no to questions. The results of these appearances were beyond the dreams of press agents, who were not noted for thinking small. In fact, these appearances even were beyond Mix's boyhood dreams of fame and fortune.

One of the unique and ingenious products of Tom Mix's fertile mind was the creation of Mixville, located on a sixty-acre site in the Fox Hills, located between Hollywood and the beach at Santa Monica. Mix had bought this estate early in his career, and on it were bunkhouses and cottages in which the cowboys who worked on his pictures lived. There Mix built a frontier village at which he filmed many of his pictures. Each building in Mixville was fully furnished and suitable for location filming: saloon, livery barn, assayer's office, and others. In addition, Mix kept a herd of fine saddle horses in his pastures there, as well as some fifty head of longhorn steers. His collection of stagecoaches, covered wagons, buggies, and other types of transportation was one of the finest in the West. In fact, everything Mix did, including Mixville, was accomplished in a big way.

As the decade of the 1920s passed, the film industry mushroomed. By this time, most of the studios had established themselves in southern

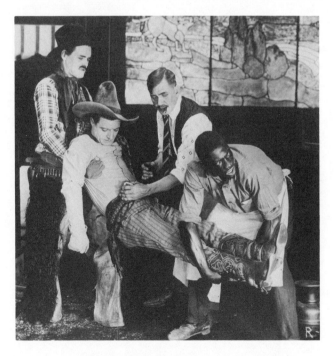

With Sid Jordan in Chasing the Moon, *1922.*

22

The Texan, *1921*.

California because of the sunshine and photogenic countryside, and the "star system" was in full swing. Tom Mix was the best-known Western star. William S. Hart still hung on in desperate earnestness, and Harry Carey had wide popularity. But no one could match Tom Mix.

Between 1920 and 1923, some of his most popular films were *Gold Coins, The Feud, The Daredevil, Cyclone, Desert Love, The Terror, The Untamed, The Texan, The Road Runner, The Big Town Roundup, Hands Off, A Ridin' Romeo, Prairie Trails, Trailing, The Rough Diamond, Sky High, After Your Own Heart, Night Horsemen, Chasing the Moon, For Big Stakes, Up and Going, The Fighting Streak, Just Tony, Do and Dare, Arabia, Catch My Smoke, Romance Land, Stepping Fast, Three Jumps Ahead, Soft Boiled, The Lone Star Ranger,* and *Mile a Minute Romeo.* One of his greatest roles was in *Riders of the Purple Sage,* for which he was paid twenty thousand dollars a week.

The release in 1923 of *The Covered Wagon* caused a greater public appreciation of the Western film. This Paramount picture was one of the first large-scale productions to use the theme of the winning of the West. Based on Emerson Hough's great novel by the same name, the film starred J. W. Kerrigan, Lois Wilson, and Ernest Torrence and was a gold mine at the box office. Parts of the filming were done in various areas of the West and utilized the elements of wind, rain, and snow to enhance the story; major scenes captured for moviegoers the epic landscape, the hazards of crossing rivers, the hostility of the Indians, and the hardships of the pioneers on the trail. *The Covered Wagon* reinforced the theme of the Western—and it reinforced Tom Mix's

The Texan, *1921.*

The Texan, *1921.*

feeling that the Western could be a major film production.

As the decade slipped past, there were technical innovations in the film industry that some people tried to disregard. Lee DeForest, inventor of the audion tube for radio, claimed that he could perfect "talking movies," but few paid him any attention at first. Then in 1926, Warner Brothers, which was in financial difficulty, seized upon this novelty, marketed by Western Electric under the name "Vitaphone," to begin filming a talkie. Meanwhile, Fox was among the first to adapt musical disks to film under the name "Movietone."

Tom Mix, like many other stars of the silent era, shrugged his shoulders at the idea of talkies. By this time he had become a master of expression and pantomime; silence suited him.

During these years Mix and his wife were living lavishly, even in an era of extravagance. Theirs was one of the great homes in Beverly Hills, a mansion using Spanish architecture; a stucco exterior; wide, tiled roofs; and an olympic-sized swimming pool. Inside were nine marble-lined bathrooms and, as Mix commented, "a butler in knee pants and powdered wig." The grounds were beautifully landscaped, while in a rambling garage he kept his assorted sports cars, several of

them imported. Douglas Branch, in his book, *The Cowboy and His Interpreters,* commented about Tom Mix's high style of living: "Such is the reward of one who has brought the flavor of Western romance to fifty million."

Richard Griffith, writing in *The Dictionary of American Biography,* noted, "Off the screen, Mix's life in Hollywood was perhaps more appropriate to the characters he played than any of his screen roles; the huge parties he gave, the jewelry he lavished on his wives, his collection of boots and hats, which would have struck a sympathetic chord with old-time cattle kings or newly rich prospectors. Hollywood's ambassador to the world, he traveled in luxurious state, something of a social lion in Europe as well as the United States."

Mix's life thus was a contradiction, but no one could deny his affection for and devotion to his daughters, Ruth Jane, born of his marriage to Olive Stokes, and Thomasina, born in 1922 of his marriage to Victoria Forde. Mix had wanted a son but, denied that, he loved his children dearly —an affection they returned. His love for them was genuine, even for a Cadillac Cowboy.

The Texan, *1921.*

Ace High, *1918.*

With Kathleen Connors, Ace High, *1918.*

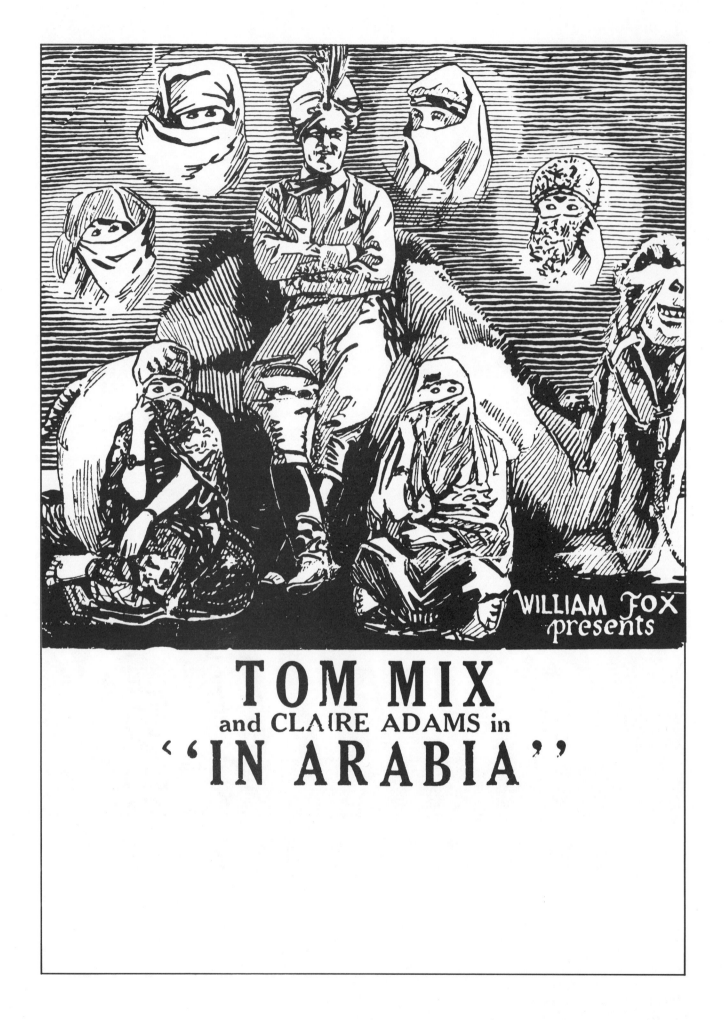

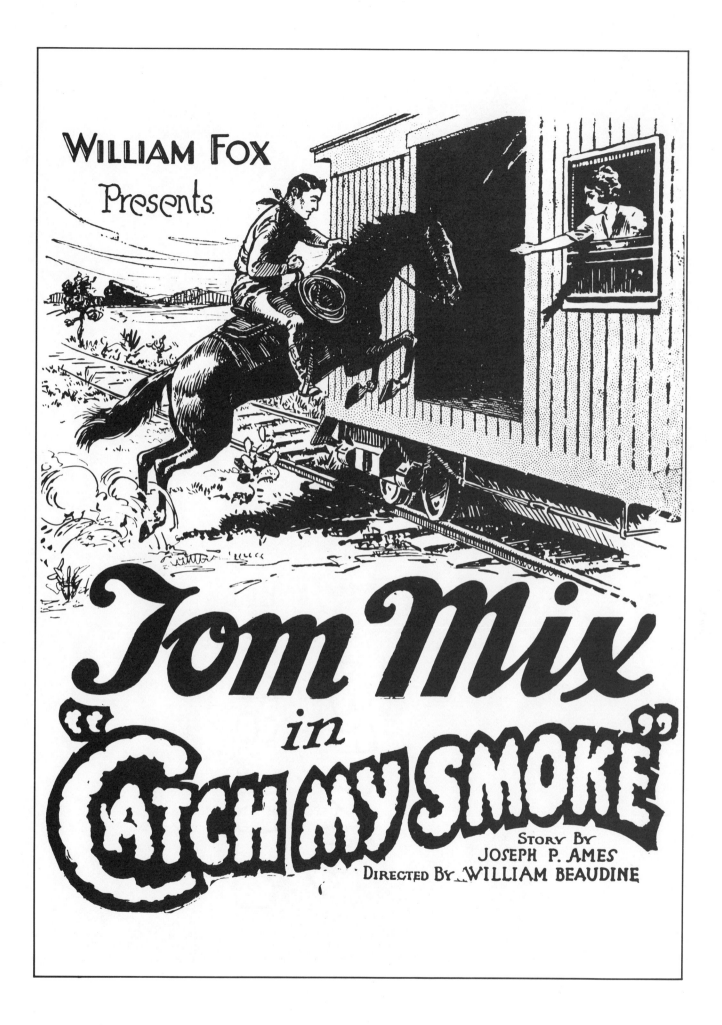

William Fox
presents

Tom Mix

Assisted by the master
horse "Tony"
in

3 JUMPS AHEAD

Story & Direction by~
JACK FORD

A tale of the western plains where the best man wins

You'll have to step fast to keep up with MIX and TONY in this high speed drama

WILLIAM FOX
presents

Tom Mix
in
STEPPING FAST

Tom Mix with Tony and his dog, Tag, 1920.

Chapter 6
THE SOUND TRACK

By the mid-1920s, Tom Mix had achieved a stardom beyond the dreams of his press agents, and his impact would be permanent. Not only did he mold the pattern of the Western movie, but also he popularized elaborate Western dress. He was the first star to have elaborately tailored suits created for him, suits that utilized tight-fitting trousers and shirts, brightly embroidered and bedecked with buttons. He also popularized fancy boots, an item of footwear that previously had been considered work wear by cowboys and cattlemen, not something for formal dress. By the time Mix finished with the boot, as one shoe manufacturer stated, "It became the fanciest thing created by God and man." Another of Mix's symbols was the ten-gallon hat. During his lifetime he gave away literally hundreds of them as gifts.

"Tom Mix always felt his oats," a friend said. "He had indomitable courage and faith in what he was doing." Indeed he did—and with good reason. During this period he was calling his own shots, giving directives, questioning scripts and, in general, overseeing every detail of his films. He was not afraid to grab a film world underling by the collar, shout what he wanted, and shove the offending fellow to the ground. Mix was strong-willed. "I like who I like here in Hollywood," he once told an interviewer, adding, "Them that I don't like can go square to hell."

The industry owners and public relations men were not offended by his tactics, for he was making good money for them. Their axiom was that any publicity was good publicity so long as the star's name was correctly spelled. Despite his great success, however, Tom Mix was dogged by marital troubles which hurt his image and his relationship with important people in the film industry. Moreover, Mix never learned to roll with punches from the press; too often he reacted to criticisms, and this made him yet more enemies.

In 1925 Mix outlined a trip that would take him through part of the United States, then on to London and Europe. This would give him an opportunity to do something he liked: make personal appearances, shake hands, give talks, and be with children. These tours he loved—the applause he received, the shouting of his name, the spontaneous laughter told him that he was still a king on the silver screen. When he set out with his entourage, it was with the pomp and pageantry of Hannibal crossing the Alps.

When he left Hollywood on March 28, 1925 aboard the Mix Special, he took with him his wife and daughter, little Thomasina, his mother-in-law, his press agents, family attendants, and grooms for Tony. His wardrobe, perhaps the largest ever assembled for a star, occupied most of one baggage car. Four days and several brief appearances from the deck of his Pullman car

later, the Mix Special arrived at New York City's Pennsylvania Station. Publicity about the arrival had brought out thousands of spectators in addition to the normal traffic at the busy station. Kids and parents watched goggle-eyed as Mix rode Tony through the large terminal where a special truck waited for the famous horse, who was given an escort to the stables of New York City's Mounted Patrol. During the next few days, Mix and Tony paraded up Fifth Avenue, momentarily stopping the wheels of the great city when Mix doffed his white hat in familiar pose and flashed a smile filled with white teeth.

Tom Mix loved this—the recognition and living lavishly at the famed Waldorf-Astoria Hotel. During this brief stay in New York City, he and Will Rogers were feted at a dinner and press conference. During this dinner, Mix reportedly commented that he "couldn't pronounce or recognize a single thing I et." Sophisticated newspaper writers criticized the cowboy star as "untutored," whereupon Will Rogers sharply defended his friend in a story that appeared nationwide. Rogers wrote that Mix was an original person with no put-on airs and that the critics were educated fools who did not know which end of a cow got up first.

When Mix was ready to leave New York City, he indulged in a unique publicity stunt, riding Tony up the gangplank of the SS *Aquitania* as a first-class passenger. Newsreel cameramen filmed this unprecedented event. Tony then was quartered in a specially built stall on the lower deck. Each day during this voyage, Mix and Tony, with special covers on his hooves, walked about the ship. Often Thomasina was on Tony's back. And Mix, ever the master showman, helped the crew of the ship during lifeboat drills by having Tony climb into one of the boats.

Mix and his family found the crossing enjoyable, but nothing could have prepared them for the tumultuous welcome they received at Southampton, England. When Mix rode Tony down the gangplank, the cheers and applause from the tens of thousands who had gathered were deafening. The high lord mayors of Southampton, Brighton, and Howe were on hand to greet him officially and to present him with keys to their cities, and he was provided a limousine and a band escort to the train that would take him and his entourage to London.

While in the capital city of England, Mix, his family, and his official party stayed in a fashionable part of Hyde Park. Tony, at the invitation of

London, 1925.

42

the Prince of Wales, was stabled with the royal family's horses at Knightsbridge. For years Mix had wanted to visit London; in fact, one of his wishes was to ride Tony through Hyde Park. This ride, long remembered as one of the most celebrated aspects of Mix's visit to London, brought thousands to the area to witness it; traffic was snarled, and the normal reserve of British crowds broke when the movie star put his horse through a series of tricks. In addition, Mix brought more cheers with a demonstration of gun twirling and roping. Recalling this round of events, Mix later commented, "It was great and beyond my dreams and expectations that the American cowboy was so popular throughout England." Mix and his family were given almost every honor in the British Isles short of being knighted by the king.

Washington, D.C., 1925.

By April 18 the party was in Paris. There, as in England, Mix and his horse were received with open arms. The pair staged a benefit performance in the Trocadero, a large auditorium, before a crowd of six thousand with the proceeds going to the Children's Welfare League. When the performance was over, Mix was presented a silver medal by officials of the French Association for the Protection of Horses. And while in Paris, he participated in a French Boy Scout enclave, was interviewed on the radio, and was featured on the front page of Paris newspapers.

From Paris the Mix party went to Amsterdam, then Berlin, with appearances in between. Throughout Europe, Tom Mix and Tony were hailed as America's greatest ambassadors of goodwill. Finally the party went to Cherbourg, France to embark for New York City. A few days later Tony followed aboard the *Aquitania* in his familiar stall.

After five weeks abroad, Tom Mix arrived in New York City looking fit and rested. *The New York Times* on May 5, 1925 chronicled the event under a headline reading, "Tom Mix Home Again—Gave Away 47 Hats." Few Americans could have done as much for the image of the United States in Europe as Tom Mix and Tony. There they reinforced the love of the cowboy that Buffalo Bill had started many years before. Newspapermen in Europe had not been concerned with Mix's grammar or his use of a particular fork at dinner; his education and background were of little consequence to them. Rather, they viewed Mix as an idol, one who represented the glorious Wild West and the frontier era of America.

Once back in the United States, Mix then set out on another strenuous round of personal appearances. His goal was to see and inspire as many children as possible. First he traveled to Boston, then to Toronto, and next back to Washington, D. C., touring orphanages and children's hospitals in each city. At the nation's capital, Mix attended the National Horse Show and dined with President and Mrs. Calvin Coolidge; during this visit he and Tony performed for the president and first lady on the lawn of the White House. At the end of the act, President Coolidge offered Tony an apple, whereupon the beautiful animal unexpectedly nodded his thanks.

Next came an appearance in Buffalo, New York, after which Mix journeyed to Detroit; the citizens of the automobile capital turned out by

President and Mrs. Coolidge with Mr. and Mrs. Tom Mix at the White House.

At the White House, May 21, 1925.

45

Tom Mix with fans attending world championship fight, 1926.

With Gene Tunney, 1926.

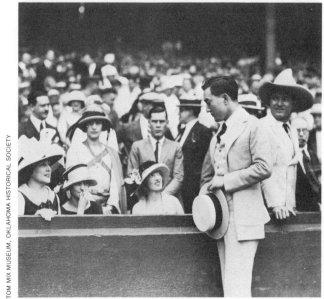

the thousands, as they did everywhere else he stopped. The *Detroit News* of May 16, 1925 stated, "Tom Mix, cowboy movie star, his wife and his daughter loped into the city on the Michigan Central this morning and are bunking at the Book-Cadillac Hotel. Mix will call on a few friends today. He announced he will leave a sombrero at each place in lieu of his card."

In a two-day round of events in Detroit, Mix and Tony greeted thousands of children, while Mix helped dedicate the Scott fountain at Belle Isle and tossed out a baseball to open a game. He visited Ford Motor Company, shook hands with Henry Ford, and commented that he preferred horses to automobiles, saying that he had never seen a touring car that could do the stunts that Tony performed. At the close of this tour, he exchanged hats with Detroit Mayor John W. Smith. Detroit would remain one of his favorite cities, and he promised to return—which he did two years later.

Appearances followed in St. Louis and Denver, ending a tour that had brought nationwide attention and publicity to Mix and the Western film. When he arrived at last in Hollywood, he and his family were given a royal reception. Huge posters and banners shouted "Welcome," while thousands poured out to see the man *Variety* had labeled "the greatest cowboy America ever produced."

Despite his trip abroad and his personal appearances in the United States, Mix made several memorable films in 1925: *The Deadwood Coach, Dick Turpin,* Zane Grey's *Riders of the Purple Sage, Rainbow Trail, Best Bad Man, Everlasting Whisper,* and *The Lucky Horseshoe.*

Productive years followed in 1926, 1927, and 1928 as Mix turned in some of his greatest performances in some of the best silent films ever made. Among these were *The Yankee Señor, My Own Pal, No Man's Gold, Hard Boiled, The Great K & A Train Robbery, Canyon of Light, The Last Trail, The Bronco Twister, Outlaws of Red River, The Circus Ace, Tumbling River, Silver Valley, The Arizona Wildcat, Horseman of the Plains,* and *Hello, Cheyenne.* This brought his total number of films for Fox to seventy-eight—in addition to the films he had made for Selig.

Yet an era was coming to a close for Tom Mix by 1928. During the decade of the 1920s, he had been the major star in Western movies, and tens of millions of tickets were sold each week as customers flocked to theaters to see him, William

Dick Turpin, *1925.*

48

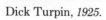

Dick Turpin, *1925.*

Dick Turpin, *1925, with Philo McCullough and Kathleen Myers.*

50

S. Hart, Rudolph Valentino, John Gilbert, Gloria Swanson, Al Jolson, and other actors and actresses. During this period the motion picture industry had begun producing and marketing something new, something profitable, which some people called "it," but which was commonly known as "sex appeal."

While Mix was making his silent films, however, one studio gambled on the new "talking pictures" by filming *The Jazz Singer,* starring Al Jolson. This film became an immediate hit in New York City, and soon theater owners around the country were clamoring to show it and other movies featuring sound (although it would be almost another decade before theaters in remote areas acquired the necessary equipment for talkies).

About the same time the radio industry was coming of age. On November 2, 1920, station KDKA began regular broadcasting, the Harding-Cox presidential election returns providing the first program material. A department store in Pittsburgh, Pennsylvania began selling receivers to a growing number of people, whereupon the Westinghouse Electric and Manufacturing Company began building transmitters. The problem of who would pay for these broadcasts was settled in 1922 when WEAF, a station in New York City owned by American Telephone and Telegraph, sold advertising time to sponsors, thereby bringing about the first "commercial."

By 1927, when *The Jazz Singer* was released, radio had become highly profitable, and there followed a struggle to merge the many small broadcasting firms into giant broadcasting systems. First among those that emerged was the Radio Corporation of America (RCA), which had been founded in 1919. Largely controlled by Westinghouse and General Electric, it assumed a commanding position not only in broadcasting but also in the sale of radio sets and equipment. By 1926 this firm controlled a chain of stations from coast to coast, while in 1927 its major rival, the Columbia Broadcasting System (CBS), was organized.

Mix at first paid no attention to talkies or to radio; nor was he worried that a new star, Gary Cooper, was looming on the horizon at Paramount. Producers gradually were coming to want sophistication in their films, not just riding and shooting. The emphasis would be on "flappers" and "playboys" and drawing room comedies. The

Tom Mix and actress Dorothy Dwan, 1926.

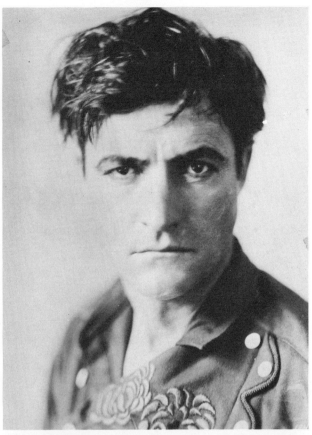

The Yankee Señor, *1926.*

The Coming of the Law, *1919.*

53

No Man's Gold, *1926.*

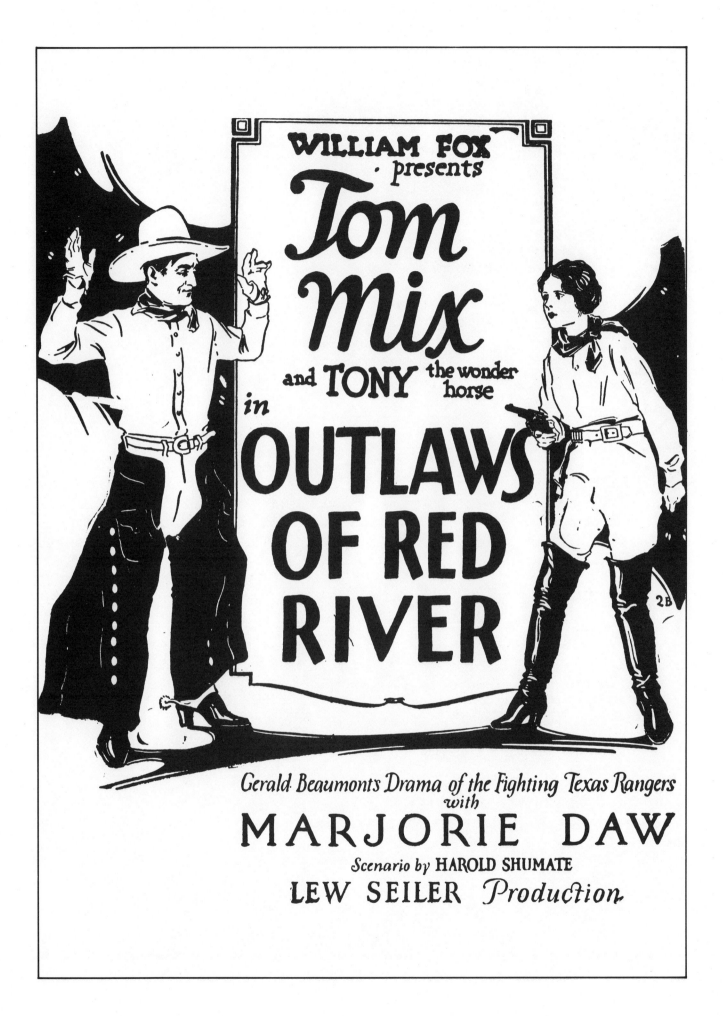

Tom Mix and Tony with the Tom Mix Circus, 1935.

With Natalie Joyce in The Circus Ace, *1927.*

world of popular music likewise reflected the changing emphasis, becoming light and melodious in such songs as "Ain't She Sweet."

This change, along with a recession that hit the West Coast and the film industry in 1927-1928, caused Westerns to be dropped by several studios, while others cut back on the number of Westerns they were making. Tom Mix, stunned and troubled by such changes, denounced Hollywood producers in *Variety,* charging the industry with poor judgment and, above all, waste and extravagance. This was followed in 1928 by

Fox Studios announcing that the end of silent films was in sight for them. The sound track had taken over.

When Tom Mix and Fox Studios parted company, the scene was as dramatic as any film the studio had ever made, yet it was done without benefit of script or camera. A few months before his death, Mix recalled the incident, "I simply nodded acceptance, shook hands with all those men, we had done a lot together, walked out to the stable, saddled up Tony, and rode off the lot . . . I never wanted to return."

Chapter 7

DESTRY

When Tom Mix walked away from Fox Studios, he was totally aware of the Hollywood cycle. He knew that stars were born in the tinsel of the film capital, but that just as surely as one zoomed to the top, so also could he fall to the depths away from the magic lens of the camera and the glare of spotlights. However, he was confident that he still had the ability to ride into the hearts of the multitude and that they, in turn, would shout his name and clamor for his heavily scrawled signature. He still had his big hat, his million-dollar smile, his extravagant clothing, and his beautiful horse. His problem was to find a place where these would be used properly.

First he turned to a small company named Film Booking Office (F.B.O.). For them in 1929 he made five pictures: *The Drifter, The Big Diamond Robbery, King Cowboy, Outlawed,* and *Son of the Golden West.* However, these never pleased him. Budgets were low—and the salary doubtless caused him to chuckle sadly. Moreover, all were silent films, and the talkies were taking over.

Then in October 1929, just short of his fiftieth birthday, came the great stock market crash. In this he reportedly lost a million dollars. Movie houses across America at first were hard hit, and many of them closed. An ominous wind was blowing, and bread lines of hungry humanity began to form like specks of ice around a freezing horse tank. If movie marquees spelled anything as 1930 began, it was hunger.

Hollywood proved quick to usher in a new trend in this era. The new productions were less serious, light escapes from the harsh reality of everyday life. With this new trend came a new cowboy image as the 1930s unfolded—the singing,

guitar-carrying troubadour. Mix realized that he was not in tune with this new reality.

Moreover, Mix had personal difficulties which were more serious than those he had encountered in his scripts. These were largely domestic and were compounded by one law suit after another. Olive Stokes Mix was pressing a law suit on him, wanting a settlement on his income since their divorce in 1917. In addition, some of his old friends brought suits or issued threats of court action in order to share in his dwindling fortune, while federal authorities were pressing him about his taxable earnings in the glory years.

During these difficulties his temper understandably grew short. Relations with his wife, Victoria Forde, thereby became strained, and another divorce would result eventually—bringing with it more publicity, scandalous in nature. One of Mix's problems reported in the press was his quick temper and his ability to use his fists. One incident given wide coverage involved Mix punching a houseguest in the nose and commenting, "He wasn't nothing but a damned gigolo." Because of such publicity, some of his fans began wondering if the Tom Mix they were reading about was the Tom Mix they had known and loved on the silver screen for so many years.

Despite these difficulties, Mix was philosophical about the past and present—and future. He had big shoulders. Outwardly he was undaunted by his problems. Although he was approaching fifty years of age, he had the bounce and courage of a young man—and he was still a master showman. Pondering his career, he decided that his charm and his ability to meet the public were major assets and that he should put these to good use by taking once again to the road. In 1930 he joined the Sells Floto Circus, determined to make

60

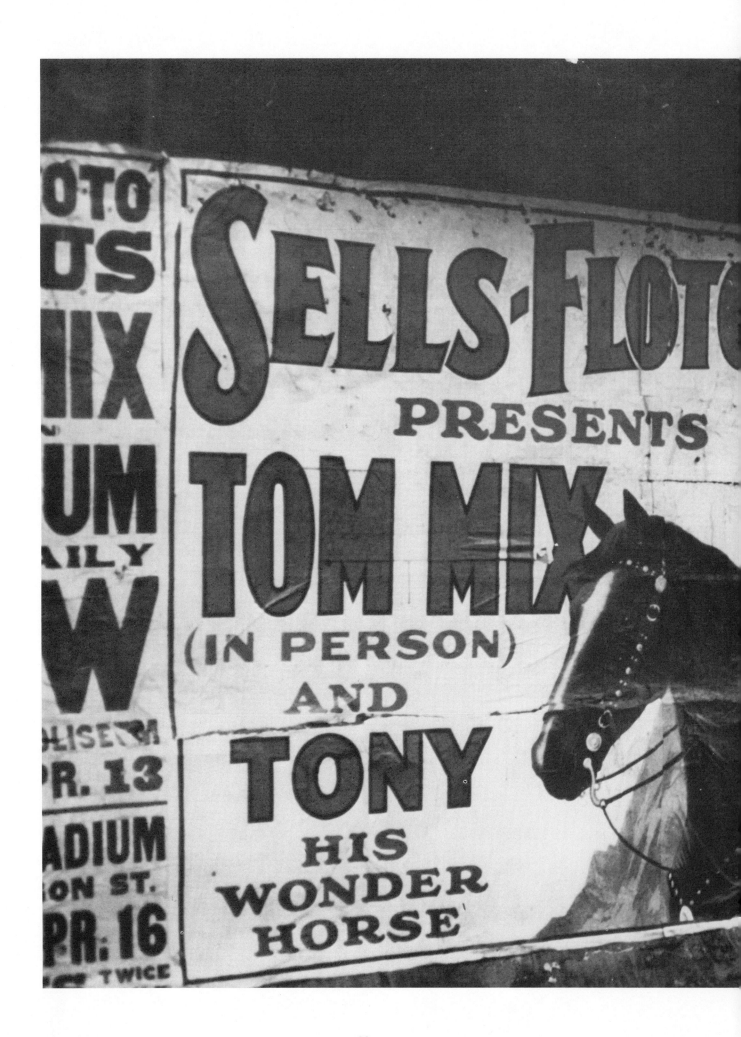

a major impact on the world of show business.

Had Mix looked closely into the history of this circus, he probably would not have signed a two-year contract. Perhaps he was blinded by receiving top billing as a star and again becoming a top attraction. The Sells Floto Circus had a discouraging history. Founded in 1902 in Denver, it originally was known as the Floto Pony and Dog Show. Later it changed its name to Sells Floto, but in 1909 it became embroiled in litigation with Ringling Brothers over rights to use pictures of the original Sells Brothers. Prior to World War I, it joined with the remains of Buffalo Bill's show with the intent of featuring a Wild West segment which had proved so popular. Nothing worked to restore economic health to the show. By the time Tom Mix joined it, Sells Floto was owned in large part by the Ringlings.

Mix loved circus life when he joined Sells Floto. There was the continual thrill of coming to a new town, the excitement of bands and crowds, and the pleasure of seeing his fans in person. And Tom Mix was good for this circus, for no performer had ever attracted paying customers like Mix. His name was magic, for he had become almost an American institution. However, within the solitude of his tent, away from the clamoring public, he had time for reflection, and his thoughts often drifted back to Oklahoma and his days with the 101 Wild West Show.

A program from the Sells Floto Circus contained an outline of what would take place inside:

THE SELLS FLOTO CIRCUS
presents
TOM MIX
in person
With Tony
His Wonder Horse

The entire, Wild West Exhibition taking place immediately after the big show is over is under the personal direction of Tom Mix. Tom Mix positively appears in person at each and every Wild West Exhibition, with Tony, his wonder horse. Tom Mix takes an active part in each and every performance in addition to directing his company of star performers. Each person in Tom Mix's Company of Wild West Stars is a champion in his class—direct from the studios of Hollywood.

Billboard at 12th and Wabash Avenue, Chicago, April 1930.

Program of the Wild West Exhibition
Under Personal Direction of Tom Mix

Display No. 1

The introductory line-up of Tom Mix, Tony, and the famous company of Tom Mix Real Wild West Stars, each a champion.

Display No. 2

Meet the world's greatest and ideal cowboy—the inimitable Tom Mix, himself, in person, and his wonder horse—Tony, the Magnificent.

Display No. 3

Tom Mix presents for your approval the famous Pony Express of the old days of the Golden West, before the advent of the steam engine. The famous Tom Mix Company will portray to you in realistic manner how the U.S. Mail was carried thru the hostile Indian country, over plains, mountains, thru storms and cyclones—with ever the one and only thought, "Nothing can stop the U. S. Mail."

Display No. 4

Tom Mix and his famous company of expert ropers, among whom are Hank Durnell, Frank Gusky, and Colorado Cotton, will now mystify you with the diversified uses to which a lariat can be attributed. Expert lassoing, rope dancing, big horse catches, rope spinning all placed before your eyes in only the way that CHAMPIONS OF CHAMPIONS CAN DISPLAY IT.

Display No. 5

Tom Mix himself now takes personal pleasure in presenting to you his famous company of trained horses, raised and trained on the famous Tom Mix Ranch in California. These horses, known as the Brewery Equines, are acknowledged as the most famous of their kind in the entire world. These horses are now being introduced for the first time—as Mr. Mix took great personal pride and care in the rearing of these horses—and personally has cared for them since their colthood days; this being one of his very few pleasures. A man in love with horses—and now you see the GREAT PALS together.

Display No. 6

Tom Mix's famous company of trick and fancy riders, led by Tom Mix himself, will now show you the expert feats of horsemanship displayed before your eyes in flesh and blood that heretofore you have seen on the silver screen in your

Destry Rides Again, *1932.*

Destry Rides Again, *1932*.

With Claudia Dell in Destry Rides Again.

picture show. These riders delight in contesting with each other and seeing which one can be the most daring. Watch them.

Display No. 7

Tom Mix and Company now present for your approval, hard riding cowboys riding man killing outlaw horses. All horses brought from the Far West under the personal supervision of Tom Mix—each having been tried and proven to be a man killer before being added to the company of outlaw horses.

LET 'ER BUCK! WHOOPEE!

Mix was a performer of consummate skill, and when he entered the arena the aches and pains of his aging body seemed to disappear. The larger the crowd, the more he responded and the better he felt. Following his act, he usually went to his tent to think or to groom his horses in silence. Sometimes, however, he would stop to laugh and joke with the circus performers and hands, especially with the forty or so in his own troupe. He still had an infectious manner, and these people were drawn to him. On rare occasions, he was sullen and moody; when this happened, he would climb into one of his cars and roar from town to town at speeds that were terrifying.

During this period he met Mabel Hubbell Ward, an attractive, lithe aerialist. Her career with the circus and her experiences in life were such that the two were highly compatible and enjoyed each other's company. In February 1932 following his divorce from Victoria Forde, Mix married Mabel Ward, and the two were happily matched.

Mix's tours with the circus increased his popularity across the country, although they took a terrible toll on him physically. Meanwhile, moguls in the film industry were having problems. Those leaders among moviemakers who had criticized Mix and the Western were reconsidering their decision. Finally high company officials at Universal Studios decided they wanted to hire Mix to make talking pictures. However, Mix was reluctant, for he was bitter at the treatment he had received—although to be wanted was like beautiful music to him. While he was considering an offer from Universal, he injured his leg when a horse fell on him. Some of the accounts of his injury were distorted to the point that he was reportedly near death. These stories brought thousands of letters pouring into the film capital, for the children of America—and their parents—wanted Mix back in Hollywood.

Destry Rides Again, *1932*.

Nothing could have been so heartwarming to Mix, at a time when he needed it, as this outpouring of affection.

Handling the negotiations for Universal was a man Mix had known and respected for years, Will Hays. It was he who persuaded Mix to try a sound picture; Mix accepted because he felt an obligation to the children of America. News that Mix was returning to pictures was encouraging to a nation in the heart of a depression. Adults felt that if a man like Tom Mix could make a comeback, then so could they—and their country. Bold headlines announced that Mix had

signed a contract and that the movies he would make would be talkies.

When Mix arrived in Hollywood to begin filming, he looked remarkably fit for a man in his fifties. Neat and trim, thanks to a regular program of exercise, he had aged considerably less than many of his contemporaries. He carried himself well, keeping his problems to himself. He was pleased to see his daughters, who were growing up. His first picture was to be *Destry Rides Again,* which was based on a popular book by Max Brand. An excellent story, it promised to be an excellent film. In it Mix rode Tony Jr. who,

The Fourth Horseman, *1932.*

68

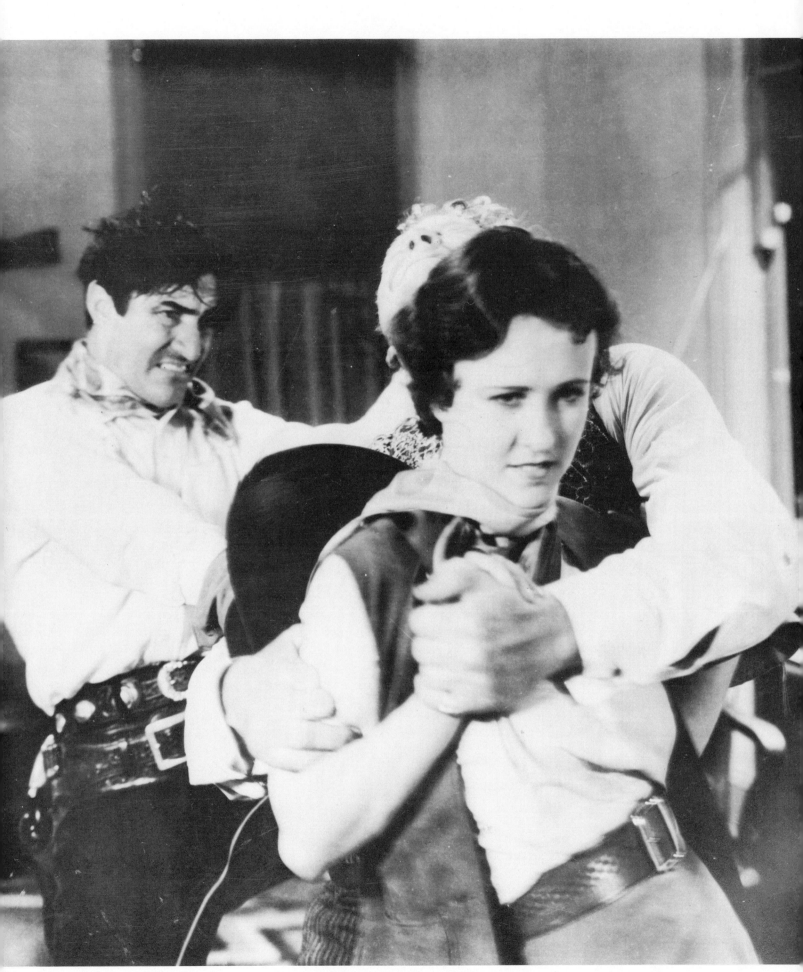

With Margaret Lindsay and Fred Kohler, Sr. in The Fourth Horseman, *1932.*

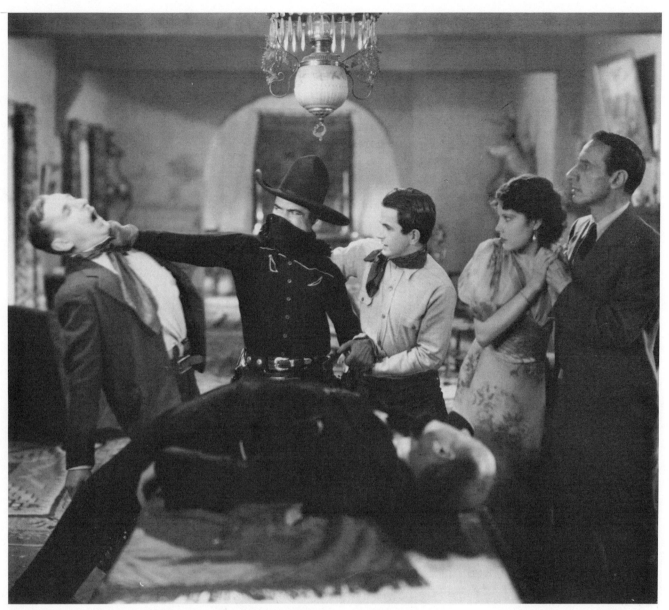

Rustler's Roundup, *with Noah Beery, Jr. (third from left).*

unlike Mix's previous horses, had to contend with sounds such as shooting, shouts, and voices.

The script for this movie called for complex action scenes involving stunts difficult for a man Mix's age. Because he had been away from films for a time, his reactions were slow, and he struggled with his lines. The months and years of emotional and physical strain, combined with the pressures of making a comeback in a talking picture, finally felled him. For weeks he lay in the hospital unable to move, while reporters implied to the public that he was in even more serious difficulty than was true. Thus he was unable to make appearances during the Christmas season. Nevertheless, he returned to complete the picture, and it was released in April 1932—which meant another round of personal appearances.

Tom later would recall that he had not been happy with the production, for he still favored silent films. The critics greeted the film with warm remarks, but Mix quipped, "Hell, I don't know who's doing the talking, me or the horse."

Destry Rides Again revitalized his career, and he needed the money. He was serious about this new career, but as usual was still plagued by law suits. These appearances in court were far more difficult than his film battles with horse thieves and cattle rustlers.

Especially troublesome to Mix was a lawsuit brought in 1931 against him by Zack T. Miller of the famed 101 Ranch. Mix had signed to appear with the 101 Wild West Show, but filming of the new talking picture had interfered. Mix had made his start with the Miller brothers of Okla-

Rustler's Roundup, *1933*.

homa and knew he owed them much. The trial came to a climax in a courtroom in Erie, Pennsylvania in January 1933; Miller was suing Mix for $342,000.

Eventually the suit was settled with a compromise, but it hurt Mix financially and emotionally. He loved the Millers and Oklahoma, but the 101 Ranch and its Wild West Show were in financial difficulty—and their lawsuit was just another example of Mix's friends trying to bleed him of money. One of Mix's friends recalled Tom saying sadly about his trials and his hours in court, "If I'd known things were to be like they are, I might well have gone to a Philadelphia law school."

Immediately after he completed the filming of *Destry,* Mix began work on a Zane Grey story, *The Rider of Death Valley.* It proved much easier for the great star for, as he said, he was getting the hang of talking pictures. Moreover, the setting of this production at various outdoor locations proved to his liking. Other pictures he made at Universal included *Texas Bad Man, My Pal, the King, The Fourth Horseman, Hidden Gold,*

The Terror Trail, *1933*.

Flaming Guns, The Terror Trail, and *Rustler's Roundup.* One of these, *My Pal, the King,* proved an unusual story for Tom Mix; set in Europe, it was designed to showcase the talents of the diminutive Mickey Rooney.

Some critics and theatergoers commented that Mix's speech in these pictures was unconvincing. In truth he had a pleasant voice easily the equal of other Western stars of the day. However, these films did not pull at the box office to everyone's satisfaction, including Mix. A new generation of children was coming to the movies, youngsters

who had grown up with radio and phonograph records; thus they were drifting toward loyalty to singing cowboys. Mix responded that youngsters seemed to be soft and advocated the rugged life for them. Gradually he was developing the image of "Straight Shooters," which was to be the hallmark of the Tom Mix radio program that would run from 1933 to 1950.

Rustler's Roundup was released in March 1933 and proved to be Mix's last film at Universal. He announced his retirement from the movie industry. However, in 1935 he would return to film

Hidden Gold, *1932.*

a serialized adventure, *The Miracle Rider,* which would bring youngsters trooping to theaters across America for fifteen weeks.

In 1934 Mix joined the Sam B. Dill Circus, a highly mobile, motorized operation which that year made two hundred and twenty-two stands. Mix, certain of his image and filled with new vigor, felt that America was beckoning. During the year, he took time out from his activities to write his old friend, Captain Frank Hamer of the Texas Rangers, to congratulate him for killing the notorious outlaws Clyde Barrow and Bonnie Parker.

In 1935 at a cost of some $400,000, Mix acquired title to the show, changing the name to the Tom Mix Circus. He directed the entire cast, putting them through a series of rip-roaring episodes that featured Indians, cowboys, and stagecoach robberies, all patterned on the theme of Buffalo Bill. Then, when the lights were turned down low and the spotlights came on, there was Tom Mix doffing his big hat, flashing a broad smile, and Tony kneeling—to tremendous applause. Next Tony would rise, after which Mix would put him through a series of tricky maneuvers in rhythm to the music of the band. Mix never grew tired of this performance for he enjoyed riding and horsemanship.

The early part of the season was pleasant. The circus began in the south and followed the sun northward to big city arenas. Mix's organization was tight and lean, but competition from big, long-established circuses was harsh. All too soon, Tom learned the economic realities of the business. In addition to the competition, he had to contend with scheduling, promotion, and the

With Patsy Ruth Miller in The Fighting Streak, *1922.*

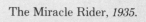

The Miracle Rider, *1935*.

The Miracle Rider, *1935.*

The Miracle Rider, *1935*.

Chicago Coliseum, 1936.

ever-pressing reality of the payroll and expenses.

During that summer of 1935, the situation was not too bad. For a time Mix thought he would break even. Suddenly, however, came the tragic announcement that his good friend Will Rogers had been killed at Point Barrow, Alaska, along with famous flier Wiley Post. The news stunned Mix, who went streaking to California filled with disbelief. Will Rogers had been a true friend to Mix, and many thoughts about the past crowded into his mind during his trip west. The two had started in show business together. He had met Olive through Will Rogers. There had been the happy days of their life together at Dewey, Oklahoma. At the funeral in Hollywood, he was lost in a crowd of celebrities and dignitaries. Rogers' death was a loss for the nation, but for Mix the loss was personal. He never would recover fully from the grief that he felt.

After the funeral he returned to his circus—the "Damn Circus," he began calling it, for it was consuming his money in large chunks along with all of his time. Nevertheless, the show had to go on, and Mix was a trooper. The year 1936 proved a good one, and Mix herded his circus across the country as he once had driven cattle. In a unique publicity stunt that year, the Tom Mix Circus crossed the country in record time, moving from coast to coast. It departed California on March 11, playing in dozens of cities en route to the East Coast. At each stop the big tent, one hundred fifty feet in circumference, was erected. After Boston, which proved excellent at the box office, he took the show south, closing at Anniston, Alabama six months later.

Because Mix was a master showman and a pacesetter, the big show owners saw him as a target and set out to get him. The competition therefore grew keener. Mix was careful in his planning to try for major population centers where he could turn a profit, but he was faced not only with severe competition but also mounting costs. Two years later, at the end of the season in 1938, he turned the outfit out to pasture. "Mix Through," the headlines blared across the country.

The weeks following the closing of his circus were bitter for Tom Mix. The big tent, the animals, the trucks—so many of the things he loved—were sold. At last all the bills were paid, and the shouting was over. Once again Mix accepted a booking with another show, this one bound for England. This tour proved leisurely. In many ways it lacked the excitement and showmanship of his trip to the British Isles fifteen years previously. Nevertheless, Tom Mix was still a "King of the Cowboys" even at his age and wherever he was.

Ruth Mix and father, circa 1936-37.

Chapter 8

END OF THE TRAIL

When he returned from England, Tom Mix spent a few days in New York City. There he was interviewed by the press, one of the longest interviews he had ever granted during his career. During the questioning, he was reflective and relaxed. Speaking about his life, he was remarkably candid, although some misconceptions about his background went uncorrected. At age sixty, he had been too successful in too many movies to admit defeat in some of life's ventures.

During this interview, he revealed that he was a generous friend to those whom he liked, but a worthy foe to those whom he disliked. For most of his success he took full credit; for the rest he acknowledged his daughters and his horses. He was incapable of certain refinements; when he was generous, it usually was the result of deliberate planning rather than spontaneous affection. Those who knew, liked, and admired Mix, and who read this interview, commented, "Tom is the same; you have to take him as he is. Either you like him or you don't." One stated that Mix was a devoted friend—but one who never lost his full measure of vanity.

Those associated with him during his last days in New York sensed a nervousness in his attitude. He seemed to be anxious and wanting. True, the world itself seemed tense, for another global war was shaping up, but as Mabel told him, it was not his war. He was too old for it, although he was still a war-horse.

When at last Mix left New York City in his big sports car, he was alone, for he was not in the mood for company. He wanted to control his thoughts, to sift them, to reexamine the future. He thought a trip from New York to California would give him ample time to think, to review his life with Olive, Victoria, and Mabel, to think

about his daughters Ruth and Thomasina.

On the way west, he stopped in DuBois, Pennsylvania, an interlude not overly pleasant. Many people there had resented his success and failed to understand why he found it necessary to project the image of a native-born Westerner. Mix knew he had done only that which was necessary across the years. Moreover, he had been generous with his mother, and he and his sister Effie had maintained the bonds of friendship. The truth was that Mix loved people and had made of himself what the public demanded. However, he had grown wary of people because of the money he had loaned never to be repaid; the total amount of money he had simply given away was staggering. In addition, there were the demands on his time, with which he was so generous that his agents and friends had grown irritated with him.

As Tom left Pennsylvania for St. Louis, where he was to meet up with his troupe for an appearance, he felt he could be proud of what he had

Tom Mix reviewing 113th Cavalry I.N.G., Camp Dodge, Iowa, August 9, 1929.

Texas Bad Man, *1932.*

The Yankee Señor, *1926*.

Do and Dare, *1922*.

The Rider of Death Valley, *1932*.

Swimming pool at Mix home in Beverly Hills, 1920-30.

Do and Dare, *1922.*

Mix with his lawyer, 1938.

achieved. From a modest and uninspiring background, he had moved to great fame and fortune. He was devoted to his daughters, and he loved Mabel. One thing he wanted to do—and planned to do when he arrived in Hollywood—was to make provisions in his will about certain items in his estate.

On October 11, 1940, he visited friends in the Gila River country of Arizona. These were friends of better days, people who were horsemen and horse lovers. Mix was extremely fond of this country, which was rich in the lore of the Apaches. In fact, Arizona had a special meaning for him, for many of his most important films had desert settings and themes. He loved the mesas, cacti, trees, and the magnificent saguaro with its upthrust arms. Often during his life he had driven out into desert, rolled up in a blanket, and slept under the Arizona skies.

Once he had met Geronimo and talked with the aging Apache chief about the desert and about the plight of Native Americans. Mix always had been a friend of the Indian, for the blood of the frontiersman ran through his veins. As he drove across this rugged country, his thoughts were about the frontier. Often he had wished that he had been born in 1840 instead of 1880 and thus could have seen the winning of the West in actuality instead of in fiction.

When Tom Mix departed from Tucson he was extremely tired but relaxed, a satisfied air about him. Along the way on this trip across the country, he had shaken hands with people who knew who he was and who complimented him. This was home ground, and these Westerners were his kind of people. A gas station attendant in Tucson said in later years that he cautioned Mix about the road ahead, saying, "There's a bridge out and some rough detours near Florence, Mr. Mix. Please be careful." Mix may or may not have heard the warning. From all indications, he did not. He doffed his big white hat signaling *adios* and roared away, leaving a huge cloud of dust behind in typical Tom Mix fashion. From a distance could be heard the resounding echoes of a powerful automobile engine revving up to tremendous speed. "I've got to be close to Hollywood come sundown," Mix had told the attendant.

Come sundown, Tom Mix was making his last ride. On October 12, 1940, the West lost one of its magnificent sons. That was the day Tom Mix died. It was a day for America to weep. It was the day Tom Mix rode up to glory.

Filmography

Selig Polyscope Company

Briton and Boer, 1909.

On the Little Big Horn or Custer's Last Stand, 1909.

Ranch Life in the Great Southwest, 1909.

An Indian Wife's Devotion, 1910.

The Long Trail, 1910.

Millionaire Cowboy, 1910.

The Range Rider, 1910.

Taming Wild Animals, 1910.

The Trimming of Paradise Gulch, 1910.

Up San Juan Hill, 1910.

Back to the Primitive, 1911.

Captain Kate, 1911.

In Old California When the Gringos Came, 1911.

In the Day of Gold, 1911.

Kit Carson's Wooing, 1911.

Lost in the Arctic, 1911.

Lost in the Jungle, 1911.

Rescued by Her Lions, 1911.

A Romance of the Rio Grande, 1911.

The Schoolmaster of Mariposa, 1911.

The Totem Mark, 1911.

Western Hearts, 1911.

The Wheels of Justice, 1911.

Mr. Haywood, Producer, Circa 1912.

Outlaw Reward, 1912.

A Reconstructed Rebel, 1912.

The Sheriff's Girl, Circa 1912.

Single Shot Parker, Circa 1912.

The Wagon Trail, Circa 1912.

Weary Goes Wooing, Circa 1912.

An Apache's Gratitude, 1913.

Budd Doble Comes Back, 1913.

Child of the Prairie, 1913, 1915.

The Escape of Jim Dolan, 1913.

The Good Indian, 1913.

His Father's Deputy, 1913.

How It Happened, 1913.

Juggling With Fate, 1913.

Law and the Outlaw, 1913.

Made a Coward, 1913.

The Marshal's Capture, 1913.

Muddle in Horse Thieves, 1913.

The Noisy Six, 1913.

Pauline Cushman, the Federal Spy, 1913.

A Prisoner of Cabanas, 1913.

The Range Law, 1913.

Religion and Gun Practice, 1913.

Sallie's Sure Shot, 1913.

Saved by the Pony Express, 1913.

The Sheriff and the Rustler, 1913.

The Sheriff of Yavapai County, 1913.

The Shotgun Man and the Stage Driver, 1913.

Songs of Truce, 1913.

The Stolen Moccasins, 1913.

The Taming of Texas Pete, 1913.

Tobias Wants Out, 1913.

The Wordless Message, 1913.

Buffalo Hunting, 1914.

Cactus Jake, Heartbreaker, 1914.

Cactus Jim, 1914.

Chip of the Flying U, 1914.

Etienne of the Glad Heart, 1914.

The Fifth Man, 1914.

The Flower of Faith, 1914.

Four Minutes Late, 1914.

Garrison's Finish, 1914.

The Going of the White Swan, 1914.

Hearts and Masks, 1914.

His Fight, 1914.

If I Were Young Again, 1914.

In Defiance of the Law, 1914.

In the Days of the Thundering Herd, 1914.

Jimmy Hayes and Muriel, 1914.

The Leopard's Foundling, 1914.

The Little Sister, 1914.

The Livid Flame, 1914.

The Lonesome Trail, 1914.

The Losing Fight, 1914.

The Lure of the Windigo, 1914.

The Man from the East, 1914.

Me an' Bill, 1914.

The Mexican, 1914.

A Militant School Ma'am, 1914.

Moving Picture Cowboy, 1914.

Out of Petticoat Lane, 1914.

Ranger's Romance, 1914.

The Real Thing in Cowboys, 1914.

The Reveler, 1914.

The Rival Stage Lines, 1914.

Saved by a Watch, 1914.

The Scapegoat, 1914.

The Sheriff's Reward, 1914.

Shotgun Jones, 1914.

The Soul Mate, 1914.

The Telltale Knife, 1914.

To Be Called For, 1914.

Wade Brent Pays, 1914.

The Way of the Redman, 1914.

When the Cook Fell Ill, 1914.

The White Mouse, 1914.

Why the Sheriff Is a Bachelor, 1914.

Wiggs Takes the Rest Cure, 1914.

The Wilderness Mail, 1914.

Your Girl and Mine, 1914.

An Arizona Wooing, 1915.

Athletic Ambitions, 1915.

The Auction Sale of Run-Down Ranch, 1915.

Bad Man Bobbs, 1915.

The Brave Deserve the Fair, 1915.

Cactus Jim's Shop Girl, 1915.

The Chef at Circle G, 1915.

The Child, the Dog and the Villain, 1915.

The Conversion of Smiling Tom, 1915.

The Face at the Window, 1915.

Foreman of the Bar Z, 1915.

The Foreman's Choice, 1915.

Forked Trails, 1915.

Getting a Start in Life, 1915.

The Girl and the Mail Bag, 1915.

The Gold Dust and the Squaw, 1915.

The Grizzly Gulch Chariot Race, 1915.

Harold's Bad Man, 1915.

The Heart of a Sheriff, 1915.

Heart's Desire, 1915.

Hearts of the Jungle, 1915.

Her Slight Mistake, 1915.

The Impersonation of Tom, 1915.

Jack's Pals, 1915.

The Legal Light, 1915.

The Life Timer, 1915.

Lucky Deal, 1915.

The Man from Texas, 1915.

Ma's Girls, 1915.

A Matrimonial Boomerang, 1915.

Mrs. Murphy's Cook, 1915.

Never Again, 1915.

On the Eagle Trail, 1915.

The Outlaw's Bride, 1915.

Pals in Blue, 1915.

The Parson Who Fled West, 1915.

The Puny Soul of Peter Rand, 1915.

The Race for a Gold Mine, 1915.

The Range Girl and the Cowboy, 1915.

Roping a Bride, 1915.

Sagebrush Tom, 1915.

Saved by Her Horse, 1915.

Slim Higgins, 1915.

The Stage Coach Driver and the Girl, 1915.

Stagecoach Guard, 1915.

The Taking of Mustang Pete, 1915.

The Tenderfoot's Triumph, 1915.

With the Aid of the Law, 1915.

Along the Border, 1916.

An Angelic Attitude, 1916.

A Bear of a Story, 1916.

The Canby Hill Outlaws, 1916.

A Close Call, 1916.

A Corner in Water, 1916.

The Cowpuncher's Peril, 1916.

Crooked Trails, 1916.

Days of Daring, 1916.

The Desert Calls Its Own, 1916.

An Eventful Evening, 1916.

A $5000 Elopement, 1916.

The Girl of Gold Gulch, 1916.

Going West to Make Good, 1916.

The Golden Thought, 1916.

The Heart of Texas Ryan, 1916.

Legal Advice, 1916.

Local Color, 1916.

Making an Impression, 1916.

Making Good, 1916.

The Man Within, 1916.

Mistakes in Rustlers, 1916.

Mistakes Will Happen, 1916.

A Mix-up in the Movies, 1916.

The Passing of Pete, 1916.

Pony Express Rider, 1916.

The Raiders, 1916.

Roping a Sweetheart, 1916.

The Sheriff's Blunder, 1916.

The Sheriff's Duty, 1916.

Shooting Up the Movies, 1916.

Some Duel, 1916.

Starring In Western Stuff, 1916.

Taking a Chance, 1916.

The Taming of Grouchy Bill, 1916.

Tom's Sacrifice, 1916.

Tom's Strategy, 1916.

Too Many Chefs, 1916.

Trilby's Love Disaster, 1916.

Twisted Trails, 1916.

A Western Masquerade, 1916.

When Cupid Slipped, 1916.

Durand of the Badlands, 1917.

Hearts and Saddles, 1917.

The Luck That Jealousy Brought, 1917.

Roman Cowboy, 1917.

The Saddle Girth, 1917.

Six Cylinder Love, 1917.

The Soft Tenderfoot, 1917.

The Pony Express, date unknown

Fox Film Corporation

Ace High, 1918.

Cupid's Roundup, 1918.

Six Shooter Andy, 1918.

Tom and Jerry Mix, 1918.

Western Blood, 1918.

Who's Your Father?, 1918.

The Coming of the Law, 1919.

Fame and Fortune, 1919.

Fighting for Gold, 1919.

Hell Roarin' Reform, 1919.

The Wilderness Trail, 1919.

The Cyclone, 1920.

The Daredevil, 1920.

Desert Love, 1920.

The Feud, 1920.

Mr. Logan, U.S.A., 1920.

Rough Riding Romance, 1920.

The Speed Maniac, 1920.

The Terror, 1920.

Three Gold Coins, 1920.

Treat 'Em Rough, 1920.

The Untamed, 1920.

After Your Own Heart, 1921.

Big Town Round-up, 1921.

Hands Off, 1921.

The Night Horsemen, 1921.

Prairie Trails, 1921.

A Ridin' Romeo, 1921.

The Road Demon, 1921.

The Rough Diamond, 1921.

The Texan, 1921.

Trailin,' 1921.

Catch My Smoke, 1922.

Chasing the Moon, 1922.

Do and Dare, 1922.

The Fighting Streak, 1922.

For Big Stakes, 1922.

Just Tony, 1922.

Sky High, 1922.

Tom Mix in Arabia, 1922.

Up and Going, 1922.

Eyes of the Forest, 1923.

The Lone Star Ranger, 1923.

Mile-A-Minute Romeo, 1923.

North of Hudson Bay, 1923.

Romance Land, 1923.

Soft Boiled, 1923.

Stepping Fast, 1923.

Three Jumps Ahead, 1923.

The Heart Buster, 1924.

Ladies to Board, 1924.

The Last of the Duanes, 1924.

Oh, You Tony, 1924.

Teeth, 1924.

The Trouble Shooter, 1924.

The Best Bad Man, 1925.

The Deadwood Coach, 1925.

Dick Turpin, 1925.

The Everlasting Whisper, 1925.

The Lucky Horseshoe, 1925.

The Rainbow Trail, 1925.

Riders of the Purple Sage, 1925.

The Canyon of Light, 1926.

The Great K and A Train Robbery, 1926.

Hard Boiled, 1926.

My Own Pal, 1926.

No Man's Gold, 1926.

Tony Runs Wild, 1926.

The Yankee Señor, 1926.

The Arizona Wildcat, 1927.

The Bronco Twister, 1927.

The Circus Ace, 1927.

The Last Trail, 1927.

Outlaws of Red River, 1927.

Silver Valley, 1927.

Tumbling River, 1927.

Daredevil's Reward, 1928.

Hello Cheyenne, 1928.

Horseman of the Plains, 1928.

Painted Post, 1928.

FBO Pictures

King Cowboy, 1928.

Son of the Golden West, 1928.

The Big Diamond Robbery, 1929.

The Drifter, 1929.

The Dude Ranch, 1929.

Outlawed, 1929.

Universal Studios

Destry Rides Again, 1932.

Flaming Guns, 1932.

The Fourth Horseman, 1932.

Hidden Gold, 1932.

My Pal, the King, 1932.

The Rider of Death Valley, 1932.

Texas Bad Man, 1932.

Rustler's Roundup, 1933.

Terror Trail, 1933.

Mascot Pictures

The Miracle Rider, 1935.

Bibliography

Periodicals

Obituary. *Billboard,* Oct. 19, 1940, p. 29.

Billboard, Oct. 26, 1940, p. 39.

Cheathan, Maude. "The Darkest Hour." *Motion Picture Classic,* July 1922.

Churchill, A. Review of *The Fabulous Tom Mix,* by Olive Stokes. *Saturday Review,* September 28, 1957.

"Introducing Tom Mix." *Photoplay,* September 1916.

Kenrick, J. N. "Tom Mix Comes Back." *Pictures and Picturegoer,* January 1921.

King, Ted. "Tom Mix." *Films In Review,* October 1954.

Lincks, Peggy. "Tom Mixes In." *Motion Picture Magazine,* February 1919.

Obituary. *London Times,* October 14, 1940, p. 7.

Mitchell, George, and Everson, W. K. "Tom Mix." *Films In Review,* October 1957.

Mix, Tom. "Advice to Husbands and Wives." *Photoplay,* June 1927.

Mix, Tom. "How I Was Roped for the Pictures." *Ladies Home Journal,* March 1927.

Mix, Tom. "Hunting With Roosevelt." *Photoplay World,* May 1919.

Mix, Tom. "The Loves of Tom Mix." *Photoplay,* March 1929.

Mix, Tom. "Making a Million." *Photoplay,* May, June 1928.

Mix, Tom. "My Life Story." *Photoplay,* February, March, April 1925.

Mix, Tom. "My Shadow and I." *Feature Movie,* April 15, 1915.

Mix, Tom. "Romance and a Hard-boiled Shirt." *Photoplay,* January 1927.

Mix, Tom. "Shaking Hands With Death." *Pictures and Picturegoer,* November 26, 1932.

Mix, Tom. "Sure, You Can Make Money in California, But Try and Keep It." *Photoplay,* September 1926.

Mix, Tom. "The Vacation Complex." *Photoplay,* September 1927.

Mix, Tom. "Wanted, Dead or Alive—Edmund Hoyle." *Photoplay,* December 1927.

Mix, Tom. "When I Faced Death." *Photoplay,* March 1932.

Mix, Tom. "Wounded Stripes of Hollywood." *Photoplay,* April 1927.

Montanye, Lillian. "The Riding Romeo." *Motion Picture Magazine,* October 1921.

Motion Picture Classic, February 1929, p. 55, 86.

Motion Picture Magazine, November 1926, p. 21, 101.

Moving Picture World, May 28, 1910, p. 900.

Obituary. *New York Herald Tribune,* October 13, 1940, p. 25.

Obituary. *Newsweek,* October 21, 1940.

Philips, Malcolm. "Last of the Cowboy Kings." *Pictures and Picturegoer,* November 2, 1940.

Remont, Fritzi. "Mixing in Mixville." *Motion Picture Classic,* October 1919.

Roberts, P. Montgomery. "The Cowboy Beau Brummel." *Feature Movie Magazine,* March 1916.

St. Johns, Ivan. "A Chip Off the Old Block." *Photoplay,* July 1925.

Thein, M. "A Short Biography." *Feature Movie,* August 25, 1915.

Tilley, Frank A. "On Location With Tom Mix." *Pictures and Picturegoer,* September 1923.

"Tom Mix and His Mother." *Pictures and Picturegoer,* January 1921.

"Tom Mix, Rider, Dies Under Auto." *The New York Times,* October 13, 1940, p. 1.

Obituary. *Variety,* October 16, 1940, p. 4.

Variety, April 22, 1959, p. 101.

Walker, Stanley. "The Western Still Rides High." *The New York Times Magazine,* April 28, 1957, p. 26.

Books

Bardeche, Maurice, and Brasillach, Robert. *The History of Motion Pictures.* New York: W. W. Norton & Co., Inc. and Museum of Modern Art, 1938.

Christeson, H. M., and F. M. *Tony and His Pals.* Chicago: A. Whitman & Co., 1934.

Croy, Homer. *Our Will Rogers.* New York: Duell, Sloan & Pearce, 1953.

Dictionary of American Biography, Supplement. New York: Charles Scribner's Sons, 1958.

Durant, John and Alice. *Pictorial History of the American Circus.* New York: A. S. Barnes and Company, 1957.

Fox, Charles D., and M. L. Silver, ed. *Who's Who on the Screen.* New York: Ross Publishing, 1920.

Hampton, Benjamin Bowles. *A History of the Movies.* New York: Covici, Friede, 1931.

Herman, Hal C., ed. *How I Broke Into the Movies.* Hollywood: H. C. Herman, 1930.

Hughes, Elinor. *Famous Stars of Filmdom.* Boston: L. C. Page & Company, 1932.

Milstein, David Randolph. *An Appreciation of Will Rogers.* San Antonio, Tex.: The Naylor Company, 1935.

Mix, Olive Stokes. *The Fabulous Tom Mix.* Englewood Cliffs, N.J.: Prentice-Hall, 1957.

Mix, Tom. *West of Yesterday.* Los Angeles: The Times-Mirror Press, 1923.

Ramsaye, Terry. *A Million and One Nights.* New York: Simon and Schuster, 1926.

Truitt, Evelyn Mack. *Who Was Who on Screen.* New York: R. R. Bowker Co., 1977.

TOM MIX
Riding Up to Glory

was designed by David E. Spaw,
photocomposed in Century Schoolbook,
and printed on Warren's Olde Style,
an acid-free paper with an expected
300-year library storage life as
determined by the Council of Library Resources
of the American Library Association,
by
The Lowell Press, Kansas City, Missouri